BENEFICENCE, PHILANTHROPY AND THE PUBLIC GOOD

Edited by
**Ellen Frankel Paul, Fred D. Miller, Jr.
Jeffrey Paul & John Ahrens**

BASIL BLACKWELL
for the
Social Philosophy and Policy Center
Bowling Green State University

ISBN 0-631-15608-9

Typeset by Katerprint Typesetting Services, Oxford
Printed in Great Britain by Whitstable Litho, Kent

CONTENTS

INTRODUCTION

Philanthropy in the Western industrial democracies has embraced an amazing variety of movements and generated institutions of great diversity. In addition to such traditional activities as support for science, the arts, education, hospitals, religion, and the poor, philanthropic activity has championed the causes of the environment, population control, zoos, and even animal rights. Philanthropy has its roots in the medieval practice of almsgiving and in the support for public buildings and ceremonies that characterized ancient Greece. And while this philanthropic tradition remains vital throughout the Western world, philanthropic practice in the United States is unique in at least two ways: it is strongly encouraged by public policy, especially tax policy, and it is highly institutionalized. There are in the United States literally thousands of private and corporate foundations and associations which annually distribute billions of dollars in charitable gifts. This is in contrast with the Scandinavian countries, in which tax policy provides disincentives to philanthropy, or Japan, in which there are fewer than two dozen philanthropic foundations, or France, in which one must secure government permission to make a significant gift to charity.

Until quite recently, there has been very little scholarly attention directed toward this pervasive aspect of American culture. But growing recognition of the importance that philanthropic activity has for society is focusing more attention on this vital "independent sector." Scholars in recent years have examined the priorities that shape the decisions of individual philanthropists and foundations and the customs and laws that regulate philanthropic activity. What was once an essentially private pursuit, albeit one with consequences for the common good, has been thrust into the limelight and is considered by more and more people to be a matter for public concern and, some argue, regulation.

The essays in this volume address a broad range of philosophical issues that emerge from an examination of philanthropy, especially as it is practiced in the United States. What is the connection between philanthropy and such traditional virtues as benevolence and generosity? What role, if any, is appropriate for philanthropy in a democratic society? What are the ethical norms that should guide the actions of both the practitioners and the beneficiaries of philanthropy? Questions such as these provide the normative background against which the findings of social scientists concerning the extent and priorities of philanthropic activity ought to be interpreted. If public policy regarding philanthropic activity will be enlightened policy, we need to be informed about the values at stake in either encouraging voluntary giving or restricting it.

One might be inclined to think that benevolence—the disposition to do good for others—is the primary motivation for philanthropy. In "Beneficence/Benevolence," William K. Frankena argues that while this might in fact be the case, benevolence and philanthropy are nonetheless quite different things. We do not ordinarily call someone a philanthropist just because he or she has a disposition to do good for others and acts on this disposition, i.e., is *beneficent*. Being a "philanthropist proper takes greater means. . .and a more formal effort." In other words, philanthropy is beneficence on a large and well-organized scale. Further, Frankena does not believe that benevolence should have the social good, in any utilitarian sense, as its object. But it is plausible, he says, to argue that this is precisely the object that philanthropy should pursue.

John Kekes is even less convinced that there is any important connection between philanthropic activity and benevolence. In "Benevolence: A Minor Virtue," he disputes the claim, made by many Christians and utilitarians, that fostering benevolence in moral agents is a good (and perhaps the best) way to encourage them to recognize that their obligation to act for the good of others extends to all human beings. He argues that benevolence is not a very important virtue, because it is only one motive among many—e.g., a sense of duty or justice, prudence, the desire to avoid guilt or shame—to act for the good of others. And generalized benevolence, concern for the well-being of *all* other human beings, is not even a particularly desirable character trait; for it may, Kekes argues, undercut the motivation to do good "in our own bailiwick," where we are likely to be the most successful.

T.H. Irwin also addresses the issue of how and to what extent we should attempt to foster benevolence. In "Generosity and Property in Aristotle's *Politics*," he explores the relation between private property and benevolence (or generosity) in Aristotle's ideal state. Generosity seems to require private property; if one does not possess anything of one's own, it is not clear that one can practice generosity. According to Irwin, Aristotle appeals to the unique benefits to its practitioners of generosity as a defense of private property. Aristotle believes that generosity is a virtue and an important component of the good life; thus, private property is justified because it makes generosity possible. However, Irwin concludes that Aristotle does not succeed in showing that private property is necessary to the exercise of generosity and, hence, he does not succeed in showing that private property is justified.

The label of *philanthropy* is generally reserved for actions which exceed in some way our obligation, if there is one, to do good for others. In "Private Philanthropy and Positive Rights," Alan Gewirth considers the issue of whether or not our positive duties to others are so encompassing as to leave little or no room for "voluntary" philanthropic activity. Gewirth argues that people have positive rights, including rights to the resources necessary to their basic well-being, and that these entail correlative duties on the part of those of us with surplus resources to help those who cannot through their own efforts secure their own well-being. In light of the extensive suffering and privation in the world, one might suppose that simply fulfilling these duties would use up all our surplus, leaving nothing for "voluntary" philanthropic activity. But Gewirth thinks otherwise. Often, what the impoverished need is not so much direct help as it is changes in institutional and social structures that would enable them to secure their own welfare. And this indicates that there is indeed a role for private philanthropy; it can help us to identify and understand the institutional and social deformities that cause privation and thereby contribute to long-term solutions to the problem of privation.

However, critics of private philanthropy often argue that it has little or no role in a free and democratic society because it is the job of the state to promote the general welfare by satisfying needs that are not met by the market and, thus, that it is unfair to provide tax exemptions to encourage philanthropy. In "The Role of Private Philanthropy in a Free and Democratic State," Baruch Brody considers three possible responses to this criticism. The first—that private philanthropy can promote the general welfare in ways that are not open to the state—he finds wanting because it is possible to doubt that private action can accomplish anything that the state cannot and because this response relegates philanthropy to a very peripheral role. The second—that permitting or encouraging philanthropy allows the state to promote the general welfare without coercion—he finds unconvincing too because it rests on the strong "libertarian" view that the state should not compel people to do good. The strongest response, Brody thinks, rests on the classical view that the state should promote virtue. By permitting private philanthropy, the state broadens the opportunities for virtuous action; and by making philanthropic activity tax-exempt, the state encourages virtue without compelling it.

But even if this is correct, there is still an apparent dilemma for philanthropy in pluralistic and democratic societies such as our own. David Sidorsky examines this dilemma in "Moral Pluralism and Philanthropy." Each instance of philanthropic activity, if it is sincere, represents some portion of the activity of "doing good." Yet, in a democratic and pluralistic society, philanthropic institutions will of necessity pursue different and even conflicting goals. This has the air of a paradox. And, Sidorsky argues, an investigation of the mechanisms that other forms of pluralism—religious, political, academic—employ to reconcile a plurality of aims with the notion of a common good does not resolve the paradox. Nor does an examination of the Aristotelian approach to reconciling a plurality of virtues with a univocal conception of the good. However, an analogy to the so-called "paradox of democracy" allows us to see that this paradox, although quite real, is not as troubling as it might first seem.

As the scope and impact of philanthropy continues to grow, it becomes increasingly important to investigate the norms that govern philanthropists and their beneficiaries. In "Philanthropy and Selfishness," John O'Connor considers whether or not there can be good reasons, other than lack of resources, to respond negatively to worthy solicitations. He argues that there can, and one of the most important is that a moral prohibition on saying "No" would undermine one of the most important motivations for philanthropic activity. Philanthropy, O'Connor argues, is often a way of expressing one's identification with a cause or an ideal or an institution. If, instead of allowing people to make their own choices, we try to motivate them with guilt, or appeals to emotion, or crass advertising techniques, philanthropic activity will soon cease to be a way of expressing such identification. This, O'Connor argues, would be counterproductive.

In "Moral Values and Private Philanthropy," Michael Hooker argues that the relationship between grantees and foundations is sadly lacking in at least one important moral value—that of candor. Grant proposals and evaluations of completed projects both exhibit a degree of hyperbole that Hooker finds unacceptable. The motivations for this are obvious and, Hooker argues, grantees cannot be expected to rectify the situation; they are faced with a prisoner's dilemma that makes it irrational for any one of them to flout this convention of exaggeration. Only foundations can effectively encourage more candor in the relationship. And they can do this, Hooker maintains, by establishing procedures for the review of proposals and the monitoring and assessment of projects that bring together the grantees, the foundations' project officers, and independent evaluators for frequent consultations.

Throughout the Western world, there is increasing doubt that government is capable of attending to all the manifold and varied needs of society. If this doubt continues to grow, it is likely that people will look to private philanthropy to accomplish what government cannot. If this happens, it is possible that the American variations on a philanthropic tradition originally inherited from Europe—variatins like the use of tax policy to encourage both individual and institutional philanthropy—might be adopted elsewhere. The questions raised in this volume are questions that we must ask if public policy concerning philanthropy is to have a firm ethical foundation.

CONTRIBUTORS

William K. Frankena has, since 1978, been Emeritus Professor of Philosophy at the University of Michigan. He has been a Visiting Professor and Lecturer at Harvard University, Columbia University, Tokyo University, the University of Washington, Princeton University, and the University of Texas. His many publications on ethics and political philosophy include *Ethics* (Prentice-Hall, 1973), *Some Beliefs About Justice* (University of Kansas, 1966), and *Thinking About Morality* (University of Michigan Press, 1980).

John Kekes is Professor of Philosophy and Public Policy at the State University of New York at Albany. He is the author of *A Justification of Rationality* (Albany, 1976) and *The Nature of Philosophy* (Oxford, 1980). He is currently completing a book on social philosophy.

T. H. Irwin is Professor of Philosophy at Cornell University. He is the author of *Plato's Moral Theory* (Oxford, 1977), and the translator of Plato's *Gorgias* (Oxford, 1979), and Aristotle's *Nicomachean Ethics* (Indianapolis, 1985).

Alan Gewirth is Edward Carson Waller Distinguished Service Professor of Philosophy at the University of Chicago. His books include *Reason and Morality*, *Human Rights: Essays on Justification and Applications*, and *Marsilius of Padua and Medieval Political Philosophy*. He is a Fellow of the American Academy of Arts and Sciences and a past President of both the American Philosophical Association (Western Division) and the American Society for Political and Legal Philosophy.

Baruch Brody is Professor of Philosophy at Rice University and the Leon Jaworski Professor of Biomedical Ethics at Baylor College of Medicine. He is currently completing a book (to be published by Oxford University Press) which explains the ways in which pluralistic moral theories can deal with hard cases in biomedical ethics. His most recent book, edited with H. T. Engelhardt, Jr., is *Bioethics: Readings and Cases* (Prentice-Hall, 1987).

David Sidorsky is Professor of Philosophy at Columbia University. His major fields of interest are political philosophy and ethical theory. Among his publications in these areas are "Contemporary Reinterpretation of Human

Rights" in a volume he edited entitled *Essays in Human Rights*; "Are Rules of Moral Thinking Neutral?" in *Mind*; and "Contextualism, Pluralism and Distributive Justice," in the first volume of *Social Philosophy & Policy*.

John O'Connor was educated at Cornell and Harvard Universities and taught at Vassar College, Case Western Reserve University, and the University of Delaware. He served as Executive Secretary of the American Philosophical Association and is currently Assistant Director for Programs at the National Humanities Center. He has written numerous scholarly articles and is the editor of *Modern Materialism* and co-editor of *Moral Problems in Medicine*. He serves as Chair of the Panel on Data Concerning the Education and Employment of Doctorate Recipients for the National Research Council.

Michael K. Hooker is currently Chancellor of the University of Maryland–Baltimore County. He is also past President of Bennington College and a former Dean of Undergraduate and Graduate Studies at the Johns Hopkins University. His research interests include bioethics and biotechnology.

BENEFICENCE/BENEVOLENCE

By William K. Frankena

I begin with a note about moral goodness as a quality, disposition, or trait of a person or human being. This has at least two different senses, one wider and one narrower. Aristotle remarked that the Greek term we translate as justice sometimes meant simply virtue or goodness as applied to a person and sometimes meant only a certain virtue or kind of goodness. The same thing is true of our word "goodness." Sometimes being a good person means having all the virtues, or at least all the moral ones; then goodness equals the whole of virtue. But sometimes, being a good person has a narrower meaning, namely, being kind, generous, and so forth. Thus, my *OED* sometimes equates goodness with moral excellence as a whole and sometimes with a particular moral excellence, viz., kindness, beneficence, or benevolence; and the Bible, when it speaks of God as being good sometimes means that God has all the virtues and sometimes only that he is kind, merciful, or benevolent. When Jesus says, "Why callest thou me good: None is good, save one, that is God," he seems to be speaking of goodness in the inclusive sense, but when the writer of *Exodus* has God himself say that he is "merciful and gracious, long-suffering, and abundant in goodness and truth," God is using "goodness" in the narrower sense in which it means benevolence, for he goes on to make it clear that he is also just and severe. Similarly, "good will" may mean either "morally good will" in general, as it does in Kant, or it may mean only "benevolent will," as it usually does; in "men of good will" it is perhaps ambiguous. My point is that goodness as a trait of a person can mean having all of the virtues or it can mean having a certain virtue, namely, that of beneficence or benevolence, though not necessarily to the exclusion of others. In short, the title of this paper could be simply "Goodness," if that term is taken in the narrower of these senses.

There are several dispositions, tendencies, or traits in the family pointed to by my title that need distinguishing, but first, still using "beneficence/ benevolence" (or, for short, B/B) in an undifferentiated sense, we must notice that there is a difference between B/B as a *disposition* or virtue and B/B as a *principle*, rule, or ideal. If one has B/B as a principle, then one believes firmly and steadily that oneself and/or others should be B/B or that it is good or desirable to be or have B/B. Having B/B as a disposition, however, does not entail believing this; one may just have a natural or motivational tendency to B/B without believing that this is good, without making any value judgment about it at all, moral or nonmoral. It may be, and I think is, true that one who has B/B as a principle also or necessarily has a motivation or some tendency to act accordingly, but then it still may be that, although one has *some* B/B as a disposition in this way, it is usually or even always overcome by other motivations or tendencies one also has, e.g., fear or self-interest. Then one has B/B as a principle, perhaps even sincerely, but one can hardly be said to *be* B/B. At least there is still a difference between having B/B merely as a principle and having it as a *virtue*, i.e., as a disposition that controls one except when it conflicts with other principles or virtues one has. In any case, to have B/B as a disposition or tendency – even as a controlling one, as Pollyanna did – does not entail having it as a principle. One may then be said to be B/B as a person, but, as we shall see, it may still be debated whether one's B/B is moral or not.

It may also be noticed that having B/B as a principle involves believing something *about* having B/B as a disposition; the two things are thus logically related, but different. I shall first say something about B/B considered as a disposition, and later something about it considered as a principle.

I

As I said, there are several things to be distinguished in connection with B/B as a disposition or tendency. B/B is not just a certain kind of action or doing, like walking; it is a habit, tendency, or trait that something has, or a way of being. Something, e.g., a person, *has* or *is* B/B. As Aristotle might have put it, one can have or be B/B even when one is asleep. Furthermore, B/B is at least two things. There is, first, bene*volence*; only persons and groups of persons, and perhaps some animals, can have benevolence or be benevolent, because this involves ways of feeling, thinking, and willing. Bene*ficence* is different; it does not necessarily involve feeling, thought, or will. The sun can be beneficent, or a climate or an institution. Something is beneficent if it tends actually to do or produce good and not evil, whether it is benevolent or not. Conversely, something is benevolent if it seeks to do or promote good and not evil, whether it is actually beneficent or not. Benevolence is a matter of intention, not of outcome; beneficence is one of outcome, not intention, though it may be intentional. Persons and groups of persons can be both benevolent and beneficent, but they can also be either one without the other. One must distinguish benevolence from mere well-*wishing* or *meaning*-well, for benevolence means *willing* and genuinely *trying* to do or bring about good and not evil; but even a person who is benevolent in this sense may by inadvertence, bad luck, ignorance, or weakness fail to do or promote good, or even bring about evil. For a person to be beneficent as well as benevolent he or she must succeed as well as endeavor, and this requires knowledge and ability or power, and at least "a little bit o' luck," but to be benevolent he or she needs only to endeavor. A person or group can also be beneficent without being benevolent. Out of self-interest one might cultivate habits of acting in ways that in fact promote the happiness of those around one. One would then be beneficent, "a good guy to have around," but one would not be benevolent. One's beneficence would be only a matter of prudent policy, as honesty is sometimes said to be.

We must then distinguish beneficence and benevolence. They are, however, connected; benevolence is a disposition to be beneficent and beneficence is what a benevolent person would have or be if he or she had the needed knowledge, power, and good fortune. Even so, a person or group can have one without the other. The question arises, therefore: if B/B is to be regarded as a moral virtue, what disposition should we take it to be?[1] We cannot equate it with beneficence, for actual beneficence is neither a necessary nor a sufficient condition of having a moral virtue. It is not necessary, because being beneficent requires having knowledge, luck, and ability or power such as a morally virtuous person may not have and need not have to be virtuous. It is not sufficient, because it does not entail being benevolent, and actual benevolent motivation and volition must be a part of virtue for any ethics that believes in B/B at all. Benevolence is then a necessary condition of having any moral virtue coming under the rubric of B/B. Is it also a sufficient condition? Here I think, the answer is "yes and no." I believe we must say that a person does have a moral virtue coming under B/B, if he or she really tries to be beneficent, whether or not he or she has much or any success at being actually beneficent, at least if that person also has B/B as a principle in the sense explained earlier. So far the answer is yes. But I also believe that to have the virtue desired in its full or ideal form one must not merely be sincerely and thoroughly benevolent; one must also have, so far as is in one's power, the other things needed for doing what, qua benevolent, one wants to do. This involves (a) having a habit of thinking clearly and logically, plus having the factual and other knowledge that is relevant to one's decisions, and (b) having at least a considerable share of the ability and skill needed to carry out those decisions, i.e., to do the good one wants to do. Borrowing a term some religious moralists have used in a somewhat different way, let us say, then, that the disposition or trait we are looking for under B/B is not just benevolence but a combination of benevolence and *responsibility*, which I shall dub BR.

One could argue at this point that the virtue wanted here is just benevolence, since one is not *really* benevolent unless one also has the practical

[1] For a similar discussion, see my "Beneficence in an Ethics of Virtue," E. E. Shelp, ed., *Beneficence and Health Care* (Dordrecht, Holland: D. Reidel Publishing Co., 1982), pp. 66–68.

wisdom and competence described, but this strikes me as pushing; "really" is *really* a tricky word. It would be better to say that the virtue wanted is just benevolence, but benevolence in its *ideal* form, or responsible benevolence, which I suppose is true. But at any rate, it is not mere or simple benevolence, even if this is understood to be more than just meaning or wishing well, and this is why I prefer to call it BR in this paper. I must, however, observe that what I am calling BR is not simply a combination of benevolence and actual beneficence. It is, no doubt, true that, ideally, the benevolent person would be beneficent as well as benevolent, but this involves his having the cooperation of fortune or providence and so goes beyond what can be required for having BR as a moral virtue. It may be that the world should be such that benevolence always succeeds, but this does not mean that success is necessary to a person's being morally virtuous or having BR.

It might also be argued that, after all, beneficence *is* the disposition we should be looking for, not just BR – that what we want and need is people who are bene*ficent*, and that, if only everyone were beneficent, no matter from what motive, we would have what we are looking for. Morality should, as far as B/B is concerned, insist on beneficence, no more and no less. There is much one could say about this Godwinian position. I shall observe only that, to use a legal expression, it entails a "strict liability" conception of morality, much like the ancient one that required Oedipus to be cruelly punished for unwittingly killing his father and marrying his mother, which has long since been given up.

II

Suppose we agree, then, that the disposition wanted under the label B/B is neither beneficence (which, though a good thing, is not a moral virtue) nor even benevolence (which, though it is or at least may be a moral virtue, is not good enough) but, rather, what I am calling BR. More must now be said about this BR. (1) Having or being BR is not the same as having a Socratic or Platonic love of the Good, for such a love of the Good need involve no love of others as such, but only a love of an impersonal Universal, Ideal, or Form, and may consist simply of a dominating desire to imitate, possess, or contemplate this Good *oneself*. Either way, it would not necessarily involve any benevolence in our sense. BR must at least include some kind of direct concern for others and for their good. (2) BR is not just love of others, for love of someone else may be only admiration or desire for that person or for that person's company; such love need involve no concern for that person's good, nor is such love any necessary part of BR. (3) Having or being BR is not the same thing as being sympathetic with others. Being sympathetic may consist merely of feeling sad, happy, or angry when others are sad, happy, or angry (or hurt), but this is not BR or even benevolence. But even if one's sympathy takes the form of benevolence, as it may, it is not yet BR, as we saw. BR, in Richard Price's words, must include a "study of the good of others."[2] (4) Does it include also a "study" of one's own good: Kant thought not, because he thought one has no duty to promote one's own good (but only one's moral perfection). About this Price wrote: "It would be contrary to all reason. . .to assert that I *ought* to consult the good of another, but not my own." But even he did not put consulting one's own good under what he calls "beneficence," which he went on to define as "the study of the good of others." There are two – or three – sides to this question, and I will say something about it later, but for the moment I shall assume that Price was right. (5) BR is not *eros* but it is also not *agape* of a Christian sort, even if this is understood to include being responsible in my sense, as it often is. For Christian love includes and consists primarily of love of God and, as God has usually been conceived, this cannot be a concern for his good, since, as Price also pointed out, "the state and happiness of the Deity cannot be affected by anything we. . .can do." Even about the Greek gods, Plato had Euthyphro say that we cannot benefit them in any way, so that our love and service of them must take some other form.[3] However, we can equate BR with responsible love of neighbor, which is also part of Christian love, but which is not always or necessarily accompanied by love of or even belief in God. Jonathan Edwards argued that, when it is not rooted in love of God, love of neighbor "cannot be of the nature of true virtue."[4] If he was right, then BR cannot be a true virtue apart from belief in and love of God, and this may be so, but for present purposes, I shall suppose that an atheist can genuinely have BR as a kind of true virtue, as it seems to me some atheists have had.

(6) W. D. Ross held that nonmaleficence is a distinct duty from that of beneficence, and G. J. Warnock holds likewise that nonmaleficence and beneficence are two distinct virtues, along with fairness and nondeception.[5] I agree that not harming others and doing them good or benefiting them are two different things, but I think that being bene*volent* is naturally understood to include both willing to do good to others and willing not to harm them. Accordingly, I shall regard BR as a complex disposition (a) not to inflict evil or harm on others, (b) to benefit or do them good, and *also* (c) to prevent evil or harm coming to them, and (d) to remove or remedy it when it does. (7) I believe that common-sensically we would regard being just to others or

---

[2] For my quotations from Price in what follows, see D. D. Raphael, ed., *A Review of the Principal Questions in Morals by Richard Price* (Oxford: Clarendon Press, 1949), pp. 140, 149.
[3] Plato, *Euthyphro*, 13.
[4] J. Edwards, *The Nature of True Virtue* (Ann Arbor: University of Michigan Press, 1969), pp. 18–22.
[5] See W. D. Ross, *The Right and the Good* (Oxford: Clarendon Press, 1930), pp. 21–22; G. J. Warnock, *The Object of Morality* (London: Methuen and Co., 1971), p. 87.

trying to promote justice among or for them as a kind of benevolence; we might cite a person's acts of promoting justice as evidence of her or his philanthropy. The Bible, however, sometimes distinguishes between God's justice and his being kind or good (in the narrower sense), and philosophers and theologians have often taken justice and benevolence to be distinct virtues, as Ross did and as Warnock does. For example, Samuel Clarke lists as the three "branches of the eternal Law of Righteousness" our duties to God, to our fellow persons, and to ourselves, and then divides our duties to our fellow persons into those of equity or justice and those of benevolence.[6] I shall likewise take BR as not including justice. BR involves seeing one's conduct under the aspect of the good or evil actually or intended to be done, prevented, and so forth, and not, except incidentally or indirectly, under that of promises kept, truth told, and so on. Justice, however, involves seeing it mainly under the aspect of how goods and evils, promise keepings, truth tellings, etc., are distributed, e.g., whether people are treated equally, as they deserve, or according to their rights. Justice is not concerned with conduct or character simply on the score of producing, preventing, or remedying good or evil, benefit or harm, but rather on the score of the comparative treatment of the persons and other centers of experience affected.

(8) Some moral thinkers, and especially some utilitarians, have maintained in effect that BR is the whole of virtue, the one and only moral virtue, the "cardinal" virtue. Bertrand Russell, for example, once defined the morally good life as the life inspired by love and guided by knowledge.[7] There is a large question here that I cannot discuss now; my own view is that there are at least two cardinal virtues, BR and justice, distinguished in the way just indicated.[8] One may then ask if BR and justice can conflict, and one might perhaps hold that they cannot, because BR is not BR if it conflicts with justice and justice is not justice if it conflicts with BR or, more generally, because two dispositions cannot conflict and still both be virtues. I find this implausible. It seems to me that, if we take justice to be or involve treating people equally or distributing things equally among them, then what is just may conflict with what does the most good and the least harm. One can still hold that, when this happens, the requirements of justice always take priority over those of BR, or vice versa, but I doubt that either view is correct. (9) The utilitarians just indicated would equate BR, not just with the study of the good of others described in (6), but with a disposition to promote, so far as one can through what one is and does, the greatest balance of good over

---

[6] See D. D. Raphael, ed., *British Moralists 1650–1800* (Oxford: Clarendon Press, 1969), vol. I, pp. 207–209.

[7] B. Russell, *What I Believe* (New York: Dutton and Co., 1925), p. 20.

[8] In this connection, see my *Ethics*, 2nd ed. (Englewood Cliffs, NJ: Prentice-Hall, 1973), pp. 41–46.

evil in the universe as a whole. Even Clarke, who insisted against the utilitarians that there are other basic duties or virtues, identified that of love or benevolence with "a constant Endeavoring to promote in general, to the utmost of our Power, the Welfare and Happiness of all Men," or with what he also called "*universal* Benevolence."[9] It seems to me, however, that, if a person constantly endeavors to do the things listed in (6), we should and would say that he or she has BR, even if she or he does not endeavor to promote universal well-being as such. Clarke seems to have thought that our taking universal well-being as such as our end in action is "plainly the most direct, certain and effectual Means" of bringing it about, but as Henry Sidgwick later pointed out, this may well not be true;[10] it may be more conducive to universal well-being for each of us simply never to do harm to those about us, always to study to do them good, and so on, than deliberately to try to bring about that end. We might coin a word and call the constant endeavor to promote the greatest general good "optimivolence" to distinguish it from benevolence. Then I am suggesting that the disposition we want under the rubric of B/B is not optimivolence, but what I have called BR. A person with BR may, in cases of conflict, choose the course that does the most good or the least harm, but he or she will not always or even often be thinking in terms of the greatest balance of good over evil in the universe.

III

Having said all this, one may still ask whether BR *is* indeed a moral virtue. I am tempted to say that, as I have described it, it clearly is one – if it is not, what is? – but things are not quite so simple. Kant distinguished between "practical" and "pathological" love, between a love of neighbor that "resides in the will" or "in principles of action" and one that resides in "inclination," "the propensities of feeling," or in "tender sympathy,"[11] and we must likewise recognize two kinds of BR, both of which fit the preceding descriptions. Indeed, we saw at the outset that one may have B/B simply as a disposition, without also having it as a principle or making any ethical judgment about it, or one may have it both as a disposition and as a principle. Thus, one kind of BR will not include any ethical belief, and so will not include any distinctively moral motivation, while the other will include both an ethical belief and a corresponding moral motivation. In Kant's sense, one will be pathological, though in no way abnormal, and the other practical. Following J. D. Wallace, I shall call the former *direct* BR or DBR and the

[9] *ibid.*, p. 209.
[10] For Clarke, see *ibid.*; for Sidgwick, see *The Methods of Ethics*, 7th ed. (London: Macmillan, 1903), pp. 385, 413.
[11] Immanuel Kant, *Foundations of the Metaphysics of Morals* (New York: Liberal Arts Press, 1959), p. 16.

latter *indirect* BR or IBR, to catch the fact that the first is not informed or mediated by an ethical judgment, while the second is.[12]

Now, Kant would say that DBR, being pathological or sentimental, is not a moral virtue, though it may be a good thing (but not unconditionally good), while IBR is a moral virtue, at least if it is inspired by the principle that beneficence is a *duty*; and the same view would be held by Price, Ross, and other proponents of what is called an ethics of duty (ED). Proponents of what is called an ethics of virtue (EV), on the other hand, would insist that DBR is a moral virtue, and at least some of them would doubt that "conscientious" or duty-inspired IBR is really a virtue at all. This is hinted at in the following lines from the poet Schiller. Referring to Kant's view, he wrote:

> Gladly I serve my friends, but alas I do it with pleasure.
> Hence I am plagued with doubt that I am not a virtuous person.
> Sure, your only resource is to try to despise them entirely,
> And then with aversion to do what your duty enjoins you.[13]

For Wallace, DBR is a "primary" moral virtue and IBR is a "secondary" one, since IBR presupposes an ethical judgment to the effect that DBR is good or right, while DBR does not. Because there is this issue between EDs and EVs, we cannot simply assume that BR is a moral virtue; this may depend on which of the two kinds of BR one is talking about.

The point here is that BR may be conceived of in either an ED or an EV way. For an ED, a disposition or trait is not a moral virtue unless it is in some essential way tied to a sense of duty; for an EV, it may be a moral virtue even if it is not accompanied by a sense of duty at all. It is, then, theoretically open to an EV to hold that, to be a moral virtue, a disposition must include or be tied to a value judgment of some kind *other* than a judgment of duty, e.g., a belief that it is good or virtuous, but proponents of EVs seldom, if ever, take this line. They really have thought that the moral virtues, however they are acquired, are or should be pathological in Kant's sense. It is not possible now to discuss the issues involved here.[14] As I see things, BR cannot be *morally* good or virtuous unless it is tied to some *moral* principle or other, and I am inclined to think that this must be the principle that BR is a duty – in short, that a person cannot be morally good or have a moral virtue unless he or she acts under the aegis of some moral judgment, and perhaps only if he

---

[12] For my citations of Wallace, see J. D. Wallace, *Virtues and Vices* (Ithaca, NY: Cornell University Press, 1978), pp. 128–131, 133, 157; see also my "Beneficence in an Ethics of Virtue."

[13] Quoted by H. J. Paton, *The Categorical Imperative* (Chicago: University of Chicago Press, 1948), p. 48.

[14] For some discussion see my "Beneficence," pp. 69–70; also my *Thinking About Morality* (Ann Arbor: University of Michigan Press, 1980), pp. 53–57; *Ethics*, pp. 63–67.

or she acts under that of moral duty. For the purposes of this paper, however, we may perhaps sidestep this two- or three-sided debate by observing that in both DBR and IBR one's bottom guideline is to be beneficent in the complex way described in (6) above. For although neither kind of BR entails being actually beneficent in those four ways, they both entail trying to do what *is* beneficent in those ways – trying to *do* others no harm, to *do* them good, and so on. As I said earlier, being bene*volent* entails seeking to be bene*ficent*. Either way, then, the thing to do is to be or try to be beneficent; whether one does so out of sentiment or out of principle, one's goal or basic guideline is the same. Either way, again, what one is to do or try to do is what the BR person would do if that person knew what to do and could do it. Having or being BR just is, in Price's sense, studying the good of others. I can therefore resume talking about BR, and will not mention DBR or IBR again.

Well, then, is BR, understood as I have described it, a moral virtue? Neither an EV nor an ED needs to say that it is but, of course, both may do so. If they do, however, they will say it with somewhat different accents. An ED will say that bene*volence* (BR) is a virtue and that bene*ficence* is a duty, i.e., that it is our duty actually to be beneficent in the sense that, if one asks what one morally ought to do, then at least part of the answer is that one is to do good to others and not evil. An EV will also say that bene*volence* (BR) is a virtue but, rather than say that bene*ficence* is a duty, it will prefer to say that beneficence is what a virtuous person would do if he or she could. This understood, let us take our present question to be: is BR a virtue, and beneficence a duty or what a virtuous person would do? Three answers are of interest here.

(1) One, which some antipaternalists might prefer, is that *positive* BR – doing or trying to do good to others and perhaps even to prevent evil happening to them or to undo it if it does – is neither a virtue nor a duty at all, but something entirely outside of the call of duty or virtue; it is no part of being moral, but a gift that one is in no way called upon to make either as a duty or even as a virtue. Even those who take this line still hold that malevolence is a vice and/or that maleficence is wrong, so that at least *negative* BR remains a virtue and/or a duty for them. It would take an intrepid or intransigent soul indeed to affirm that it is not.

(2) A second answer is to agree that positive BR is neither a duty nor a virtue that is required of everyone at least to some extent, or even of everyone capable of doing any good to others; it is not something the absence or neglect of which is in any way morally wrong, bad, blameworthy, or culpable. However, it still has moral standing; it is something some persons ought to have or be; it is indeed a moral virtue, but it is a supererogatory one, something that is morally right, good, or praiseworthy even if what it leads

one to do is beyond the call of duty. It is, in fact, something that idealistic individuals and those blessed with the means of doing good may themselves see as a duty even if others do not, and even if they would in no way be morally bad or in the wrong if they were to beg off.

(3) The third view is to hold, as Kant and J. S. Mill have, not only that BR is a virtue, but also that positive beneficence is a duty and neglect of it wrong or vicious, and then to add that it is not a strict or perfect duty but a wide or imperfect one.[15] There are problems about this position, to which I shall return, but what Kant and Mill had in mind is that at least some helping of others who are in need is a duty, and that failure ever to help anyone even when one can is wrong, bad, and blameable, even if not doing good at every opportunity one has is not. One has, they thought, some leeway in the matter of when and where to try to do good, for whom, and in what way. They also held that beneficence is a duty to which there is no correlative right that any particular individual has, as A has a right to B if I promise B to A. *Some* good Samaritanism at least is morally demanded of one, if one is able to do it at relatively little cost to oneself, though others have no right to it even then (unless one stands in a certain relation to them, e.g., that of being their father or mother).

I find the hard line taken in the first position impossible to believe; both of the other positions, which say yes to our question, seem to me much more plausible. Indeed, I think the second and third should be combined in a recognition that there is an area in which positive BR is a required virtue and positive beneficence a duty, if only an imperfect one, and another area in which it is not required but is still morally desirable and not simply a gift that is morally indifferent. I am even inclined to go beyond the third view and to hold that in some situations another person has a right to expect me to help him or her even if I am not a friend or a relative and am not required to help by any office or role. In any case, it seems to me that there is a burden of argument on anyone who takes the first view that positive BR is not a moral virtue, or that BR calls *only* for nonmalevolence or nonmaleficence.

One more point here: Plato distinguished between justice as a virtue of an individual soul and justice as a virtue of the state, and one might likewise distinguish between BR as a disposition or virtue of a person and BR as a disposition or virtue of a state. In these terms, I am dealing with the former rather than the latter, since our subject here is *private* philanthropy. I do think, however, that BR can be a virtue either of an individual doer of good or of a group of individuals cooperatively engaged in doing good, and so even of nations of people. As for *institutions*, I take it that as such they cannot be or

---

[15] See Kant, *Foundations*, p. 39; J. S. Mill, *Utilitarianism* (New York: Liberal Arts Press, 1949), p. 53.

have BR, because they cannot exercise *volence* and therefore not benevolence. They can and should, of course, be beneficent.

IV

Thus far I have been dealing with B/B as a disposition, and especially with BR, which I take to be the disposition involved in or motivating private philanthropy. Now I must say something about B/B as a *principle*. Having it as a principle is believing seriously and steadily that one is to be bene*ficent* in four ways, either because beneficence is a duty or because benevolence (BR) is a virtue and beneficence is one of the things a virtuous person would do. In short, one believes in what in my little book *Ethics* I call the principle of beneficence and takes it as one of one's basic guides to action, in either an ED or an EV way. How does or should this work out in one's life? Two classical discussions of this are Cicero's in *De Officiis* and Seneca's in *De Beneficiis*, and it would be interesting here to review what they said; but I prefer to go over the same subject in my own way, rather more briefly, and without dealing with gratitude, which played an important part in their thinking about beneficence but plays little in mine.

As I see it, the principle of beneficence (PB) tells us four things:

(a) not to bring or inflict evil or harm on others,
(b) to benefit or do them good,
(c) to prevent evil or harm coming to them, and
(d) to remove or remedy it when it does.[16]

Notice, it does not tell us what we should do if following these instructions brings us into conflict with other basic moral principles, e.g., with the principle of justice, which I take to be that of treating people equally. This is not something the PB itself can tell us; it cannot determine its own place in the moral economy. On this question, to venture only one remark, it seems to me that considerations of justice do not always take precedence over those of beneficence, as Cicero thought, and also that those of beneficence do not always take precedence over those of justice, as some utilitarians think. I have also suggested that the PB does not tell us simply or straightaway to do what will promote the greatest general balance of good over evil (or the social good so understood), as some utilitarians think it does. That is what the principle of utility, understood as an act-principle, tells us. The PB tells us something more ideal, less compromising – that we are to do *no* evil, to bring *only* good to others, and so on. Also, it does not assume that goods and evils can be measured and balanced against each other as the principle of utility does; it does not deny that this is so, but it is compatible with the view that

16 See my *Ethics*, p. 47.

goods and evils may differ in quality and not just in quantity. It could allow, for example, that, if act A produces 99 units of good and no evil, while act B produces both good and evil but yields a net balance of 100 units of good over evil, then A is the right thing to do, not B, as the principle of utility requires us to say. This is why the PB seems to me preferable to that of utility as a basic principle of morality and beneficence. Indeed, it also seems to me that the principle of doing what will bring about the greatest available balance of good over evil is plausible only if and when it is not possible to do what the PB asks of us, and that in this sense the principle of utility rests on the PB. Producing the greatest balance of good over evil cannot be the ideal thing to do; it can only be the best thing to do in practice.[17]

In any case, it must, of course, be recognized that in practice two of the instructions of the PB may come into conflict; it may be that doing good in a certain situation entails also doing harm, or that avoiding doing evil also entails missing doing good, or even that every action open to us entails doing both good and evil. For many such situations one solution would be to insist that instruction (a) always takes precedence; one is never to bring harm or evil to anyone, no matter what or how much good is lost to others because one avoids doing so. For the special case in which one cannot avoid bringing about evil, no matter what one does (even if one "does nothing"), the corresponding solution would be to say that one should always do what will bring about the least evil, no matter what the cost is in terms of the good one might do. But these solutions, it seems to me, cannot be derived from the PB itself. As far as that principle goes, it seems more plausible to say that in the sorts of situations envisaged one is permitted, if not instructed, to do some harm if this is necessary to achieve much good (at least if doing the harm is not itself a means to doing the good, but only an unavoidable accompanying outcome), or even to do what will bring about the greatest balance of good over evil.

It is said that in such situations one is never to do evil that good may ensue. This raises interesting questions I cannot go into, but I should point out that the injunction involved is ambiguous. "Jones does evil" may mean "Jones does an action that is morally wrong or morally bad." Here the evil done is the action itself, not just its result. Or "Jones does evil" may mean "Jones causes something bad to happen to someone (e.g., an injury, pain, or suffering)." Then the evil done is not Jones's action itself but its result. The injunction cited may then be saying either of two different things: (a) that one is never to do an action that is morally wrong or morally bad in order to bring about a good result, or (b) that one is never to cause something bad, e.g., pain, to happen to anyone in order to bring about a good result, e.g., an

---

[17] ibid., pp. 45–46.

increase in general happiness. In (a) the action in question is by definition morally bad or wrong, but in (b) it is not – its being wrong is an open question. Now, simply as it stands, even (a) can be doubted, but in what I was saying it is (b) that I was questioning, and I may add that (b) cannot merely be assumed to be true, as it often is by those who support the injunction cited, since its truth is precisely what is at issue between them and their opponents.

V

Another problem with the PB in some eyes is that, as it stands, it seems to ask too much – that we do *no* evil, that we *always* do what good we can, or at least that we *always* do what will bring about the greatest general balance of good over evil. There is so much good to be done in the world and so much evil to prevent or eliminate that one hardly knows where to begin and can see no end, and cannot take any break along the way. One has no option but to be beneficent and no freedom about how or when to be. Moreover, there is the concert ticket kind of case. Suppose I have a ticket to a certain concert and someone else shows up who wants but cannot obtain one. By the PB am I not required to give her mine? I can do so without any cost to myself except missing the concert, and perhaps she needs to hear it more than I do or will get more enjoyment out of it. If so, can it be right for me to keep the ticket for myself to use, as we usually think it is?

One question here is whether it is always only *others* that the PB requires or permits us to consider in any way. I raised this in (4) of section II, citing Kant and Price, and saying I would come back to it. Though I have some sympathy with Kant's position, I think, as Price does, that the answer is that the PB need not be understood in a purely altruistic or other-regarding sense; it can be seen as saying that we are to do good, not do evil, and so on, to any person or conscious sentient being as such, and thus as applying to oneself as well as to others. Then it allows one to consider oneself, though not just because one is oneself but only because one is a person or conscious sentient being. It may still require me to give another the ticket if the concert would mean more to her than to me, but at least it permits me to keep it if the concert would mean as much or more to me. More about this later.

To return to our problem, one may, of course, take the position that the PB *does* ask all that it is represented as asking of us, and that it is right in doing so. The Christian ethic of love sometimes seems to take this position. But there are other responses one can make to critics of the PB. (A) If one believes, as I do, that there are other basic principles of morality besides the PB, e.g., a principle of justice, then one can say that sometimes one may do less than the PB asks because another basic principle requires one to. In Ross's terms, one can hold then that beneficence is a prima facie, not an absolute duty; when some other prima facie duty applies and takes precedence, then the PB is overridden. (B) It can also be pointed out, as it was by Cicero and Kant, that one can be required only to be as beneficent as one can be. Ought implies can. What one can't do isn't "oughty," and so not doing it isn't naughty. Here, however, we must notice that there are cans and cans. There are things I simply *cannot* do in the way of being beneficent, like giving $1,000,000 to charity; and there are things I *could* do but only at great cost to myself, but which might still be for the greatest general good, e.g., giving to charity everything I do not really need. I might say then, "But I can't do that. It is too much to expect." Strictly I could, but less strictly I cannot. We do often say somebody cannot do something when we mean only that he or she cannot rightly be expected to. It is, of course, true that one has no duty to help someone when one strictly *cannot* do so, and perhaps it is also true that one has no duty to do so when one *can* but cannot rightly be expected to, but then we still need some way of determining when it is right to expect one to help or to be otherwise beneficent. One can get some mileage out of this point, but it is not clear how much.

(C) It can also be argued that there are other circumstances in which one may depart from being beneficent. For example, one may have to take off from being beneficent in order to acquire the means to be beneficent with, say to acquire money or a skill; or one may even have to relax in order to recreate or refresh oneself for going on in one's do-gooding. All work and no play make Johnny a dull benefactor, you might say. So one may even take a holiday! In fact, it may even be that the PB itself requires one to. (D) Following Bernard Williams's lead, a Gauguin might beg off being beneficent by pleading that, being what he is, there is something else he simply *has to* do: go to the South Sea Islands to paint pictures.[18] And he may offer this either as an excuse for not being beneficent even though he ought to be, as an argument to show that it is morally all right for him to take off and paint, or as a compelling reason for his not doing what he morally ought to do. I am not sure what to think about such pleas on his part, and will only observe that in the first two cases it is not clear that morality should recognize his plea, and that in the third he would be taking a point of view outside of it.

To deal further with the problem one might take the line that beneficence is an imperfect or wide duty in the sense indicated earlier. Then one does not always have to be making like a benefactor, even when one can and it is consistent with the other basic principles of morality. One has some playroom, as Kant put it, and this does not mean only that one may play when recreation is needed for one to go on being beneficent or even that one can take some time to acquire the means for going on; it means also that one has

---

[18] B. Williams, *Moral Luck* (Cambridge: University of Cambridge Press, 1981), pp. 22–25.

moral options about how beneficent to be, when, or toward whom. I think this line may well be the right one to take, and it would do a good deal to meet the objection that the PB asks too much, especially if it were combined with the line described in (2) of section III. I am, however, uncertain about just how to justify it against both the view that beneficence is a perfect duty and the view that it is no duty at all.

There is, nevertheless, more to be said, namely, that the above problems arise *if* the PB is regarded as being mainly or wholly an *act*-principle, i.e., as a principle for individuals to act by in the sense of always asking in each situation what *it* requires one to *do* in that situation. It might, however, be regarded as mainly or wholly a principle for determining what more concrete *rules* to live by or what more specific *dispositions* to foster in oneself and others, rather than as a principle for determining what particular *acts* to perform. Then one would always or mostly decide what to do by reference to the rules or dispositions determined on, and not by appeal to the PB itself. Yet, since those rules and dispositions are selected because of their beneficence or beneficiality, one would still be guided basically by the PB, only indirectly rather than directly. Rule utilitarians and other indirect utilitarians have sometimes taken such a view of the principle of utility, and one can take a parallel view of the PB.

This direction of thought has a good deal to be said for it, and can be made more concrete as follows. Societies have generally had, in addition to a legal system and a set of etiquettical conventions, what is called a positive social morality (PSM), i.e., a set of moral rules, ideals, and values that are taught in the society and supported by external sanctions like blame and praise and by internal sanctions like feelings of conscience. Roughly, a PSM is like both etiquette and law, and somewhere between them, more serious than the former and less formal or official than the latter. Moreover, it can plausibly be argued that a society should have a PSM or quasi-legal system of this sort, i.e., that morality is not and should not be a purely personal business in which each individual is left to her or his own devices in the matter of being beneficent, just, etc.[19] Ideally a PSM should be such that, if its rules and precepts are generally taught, sanctioned, and followed, then life for the members of the society (and for others) will be better and more just than it would be without any PSM or with any alternative one. Notice here that a PSM is justified not only by its beneficence but also by its justice, by what pattern of the distribution of goods and ills its prevalence issues in. Perhaps any actually prevailing PSM may be presumed to be better than none or even to be at least tolerably beneficent and just but, of course, it may

[19] See my "Is Morality a Purely Personal Matter?" *Midwest Studies in Philosophy*, vol. III (Morris: University of Minnesota Press, 1978), pp. 122–132.

still also be unideal in important respects. Any society or individual that believes in beneficence and justice must keep trying to see that the prevailing PSM is as beneficent and just as possible. If it is, then the individual may normally be guided by its precepts and rules rather than directly by the principles of beneficence and justice themselves. However, one may sometimes find oneself in a kind of situation in which it seems clear that acting on the rules of one's PSM is antibeneficent (or unjust) in a serious way, and then one may have to decide to go it alone directly in the light of the PB (etc.), besides, of course, working to improve the PSM.

My point is that, where the PSM is right or nearly right, an individual can be guided by its precepts rather than by the PB (etc.), because then doing so is justified by the fact that the result is generally beneficial and just. If this is so, then the BR person need not always have his or her eye glued directly to the social good, but may and should look to the social good through the prism of a well-constructed PSM and other institutions. Thus, indirect utilitarians, rule utilitarians, and even some act utilitarians have argued, against critics of utilitarianism, that the BR person need not always or usually stand entirely naked before the PB asking it what to do, though he or she may have to do so on occasion. I believe that this view of the matter will do much, though not everything, to bypass the problems mentioned earlier and has a considerable plausibility in itself. For example, one could perhaps argue that the best PSM for our society to have would include a rule permitting me to keep the concert ticket even when someone else would benefit more from having it.

There will, of course, be occasions for which such a PSM does not, and perhaps should not, provide rules guiding the BR person or the would-be private philanthropist. Even then a society can do things to help guide them in their beneficence. It can set up other institutions and organizations through which they can channel it. For example, the family can be viewed as such an institution; at least when it is functioning ideally, then, other things being equal, individuals can direct their beneficence primarily toward relatives and leave members of other families to their relatives, and expect that everyone will come out cared for (and justly treated). Perhaps the same thing can be said about the institution of nationhood. The law also, by way of its regulations, can help individuals to be beneficent, e.g., by providing for the making and execution of wills. Of course, the family and the nation often fall tragically short of achieving the ideal just indicated, as in the cases of Appalachia, Bangladesh, and Ethiopia, and then society can and should provide channels through which private individuals and groups can implement their beneficence, e.g., ways in which private members of a more fortunate family or nation can exercise beneficence toward those of less fortunate ones. Even a government and its officers may help private benefactors in this way by creating national and international agencies through which they can work. Of course, they may also themselves act directly to benefit their people or those of other countries, but such philanthropy will not be private.

VI

It would seem that, both in connection with BR as a disposition and with beneficence as a principle, one must go on to address the question: what is the good and what bad? Once again, however, things are not quite so simple. (A) In view of the above, we may characterize the BR person as trying to affect the incidence of good and evil in the lives of others in four ways. It seems to follow that BR entails one's having some judgment about what *is* good and what bad. But we may still ask whether one is to do to others what one *believes* to be good and not bad or what actually *is* good and not bad. A plausible answer is that ideally one should do what actually is good and not bad, i.e., be bene*ficent*, but that in practice one is never in a position to choose between what one believes to be good or bad and what is good or bad, so that one can only go by one's judgment about such things. Of course, one's judgment may be mistaken, but this only means that one should be as careful and reflective about one's value judgments as possible; in fact, this is part of what it is to be responsible in one's benevolence, and no more can be asked. (B) However, some people would respond that one should not or may not go by one's own judgment about what is good or bad for others, no matter how careful and reflective it is; rather, one must go by what *they* judge to be good or bad for them. Paternalism has come under heavy attack in recent decades, and some of its critics have taken rather extreme positions against it. Even Kant wrote, in discussing this "casuistic" question, that "I cannot do good to anyone according to *my* concept of happiness (except to young children and the insane), but only according to that of the one I intend to benefit."[20] If this is true, then my being or having BR does not require me to have sound judgments about what is good or bad for others, for I have only to go by *their* judgments. But there are obvious limits to this, as Kant admits, and it is not clear that they obtain only in the case of young children and insane people; in any case, Kant would not think it right to do to another what one is sure is bad for him or her. What concerned him was the kind of paternalism that involves violating another's freedom or right to freedom; respect for another's right he regarded as a side-constraint even on one's efforts to be beneficent, but this does not mean that beneficence itself is merely a matter of doing to others what they take to be good and not bad for them, whether one believes they are right about this or not. Kant is saying

[20] Immanuel Kant, *The Doctrine of Virtue* (New York: Harper and Row, 1964), p. 122.

that duties of respect for freedom and rights take precedence over those of love or beneficence, not that beneficence is not a study of the good of others. He does say that beneficence consists of making others' ends one's own if those ends are not immoral, but in practice he equates this with helping others according to our ability when they are in need, and this need not mean merely helping them when they *think* they are in need.

(C) We have it on good authority that one is to do to others what one would want them to do to one. This so-called Golden Rule has been criticized by many, including Kant, but taken literally it too means that BR does not require one to make judgments about what is good or bad, but only judgments about what one does and does not want others to do to one. It may still be a useful rule of thumb, but whether or not one should always follow it would seem to depend on what it is that one wants others to do to one, and it may be that what one wants them to do is not what is good for one or what they should do. Simply as it stands, the rule's goldenness is hardly solid.

I still believe, then, in spite of the considerations just mentioned, that, if we mean to push BR as a virtue, we must also push the study of what *is* good or bad for others, not just that of what they judge good or want or that of what we want. We must recognize that, in striving to be beneficent, we should be careful not to neglect other moral requirements, but this does not mean that we can proceed without trying to form sound judgments about good and evil. And, as for the requirement to respect others' freedom, if we take freedom to be a great good, we may hold that BR itself requires us not to let our pursuit of the other goods of others interfere with their freedom. The same can be said about the requirement to honor others' need for self-respect.

If what I have now been saying is anywhere near correct, then a full essay *de beneficiis* must after all include a theory of good and evil. At the very least, it should do what it can to enlighten the wants and value judgments both of would-be benefactors and of those they mean to benefit. Here, however, I shall not try to provide such a theory.[21] Two remarks must suffice. One is that, in seeking to be beneficent, we may perhaps normally take as goods to be brought about and evils to be avoided or remedied those things about which there is a consensus among reflective people in the culture or cultures involved. This may not always be reliable, and in the crux one may have to act on one's own best judgment but, provided that we remember the dangers of paternalism, it will be better than simply going by one's own unchecked judgments or the unchecked judgments of those we are trying to benefit. Of course, what is thus seen as good or bad varies from culture to culture – from

---

[21] I do something in that direction in *Ethics*, ch. 5.

a secular culture to a religious one or from one religious culture to another – and this is something a would-be benefactor must remember, but it does not mean that what is beneficial and what not is entirely defined either by his or her culture or by that of those he or she seeks to benefit. The other remark is that, in any case, it is for most philanthropical purposes clear enough what is good or bad, e.g., that food, clothing, shelter, health, and education – and lots of other things – are good and their absence bad.

VII

Now, finally, a little about private philanthropy and the social good. The former I take to be philanthropy done by individuals or groups in their private capacities; it may be publicly done, as well as privately or secretly, but one cannot do *private* philanthropy in one's capacity as a public or governmental officer or servant, nor even, I think, in one's capacity as an officer of a philanthropical organization, at least if one makes one's living by what one does as such an officer. The head of a foundation who is employed to give money away to charitable causes is not as such a true private philanthropist, however much he or she may be moved by BR, but the wealthy person who employs such a head may be one. As for the social good, this should, I believe, not be understood simply as the greatest general good, the greatest general balance of good over evil, of happiness over unhappiness, of welfare over illfare, of pleasure over pain, or of satisfaction over dissatisfaction, as it so often is. Something about the pattern of distribution has to come into the conception – something about whether more people are benefited rather than fewer and about whether the distribution is just or equal or not. The classic phrase "the greatest good of the greatest number" catches some of this. It would be even better, to my mind, to describe the social good as that state of affairs in which everyone has the best life of which she or he is capable. At any rate, something about justice must come in, not just something about quantities of good and evil.

Now, in a way, what I have been discussing is private *philanthropia*, though with almost no reference to the social good as such, but in a way I have not been discussing private *philanthropy* at all. What I mean is this: we must distinguish between private philanthropy proper and private BR in the broad sense in which I have been talking about it. The latter is or should be motivated or generated by benevolence (or by more specific dispositions like fidelity that are selected and cultivated because of the beneficiality of our having them), and consists simply of trying to be beneficent, directly or indirectly, in one's relations to others. But we would not call just anyone who is or tries to be beneficent in daily life a philanthropist; we reserve this label for someone who has BR in a special way or to a special, possibly to a supererogatory, extent. BR in the wider sense may include giving to charity, but it need not; the widow in Mark's story might not even have had a mite to give and yet had BR. Being a private philanthropist proper takes greater means, either one's own or provided by others one enlists, and a more formal effort. Also, I think, such philanthropy need not be motivated by BR in any significant way, though I suppose it normally is; we would call a person who contributes to and works for philanthropical causes a philanthropist, at least in a funeral eulogy, even if that person is or was moved, not by BR, but by a desire for public esteem or political ambition.

We must then distinguish between a more run-of-the-mill kind of BR and its exercise in life and private philanthropy proper. I now wish to suggest, in conclusion, that there may be a further difference in their relations to the social good. I argued earlier that B/B in the broad sense does not necessarily and should not normally have the social good in general as its pillar of cloud by day and its pillar of fire by night. It may be, however, that private philanthropy proper should take the social good, as I just roughly defined it, as its guiding pillar in the world, though perhaps not without understanding that it too must respect the freedom and self-esteem of those being bene-fited. Hopefully, both private B/B of the ordinary kind and private philan-thropy proper will have as a *result* an advance in the social good, if they are responsible in my sense, but, perhaps the latter may or even should con-stantly take the social good as its explicit *goal* or *target*, even though the former need not and should not.

Philosophy, University of Michigan

BENEVOLENCE: A MINOR VIRTUE

By John Kekes

I

Morality requires us to act for the good of others. This is not the only moral requirement there is, and it is, of course, controversial where the good of others lies. But whatever their good is, there can be no serious doubt that acting so as to bring it about is one crucial obligation morality places on us. Yet the nature of this obligation is unclear, because there are difficult questions about its aim and about the motivational sources required for realizing it. Who are the others for whose good we are obligated to act? Are they only people in our immediate context, or members of our society, or all human beings? And, as a matter of moral psychology, what leads us to honor this obligation? Is it a sense of justice, decency, prudence, benevolence, or some combination of these and perhaps other virtues? The answers we give will shape our understanding of the nature of the obligation. For the character traits which we think should move us will influence the choice of people we aim to benefit and the inclusiveness we attribute to the obligation will affect the motives we wish to cultivate in ourselves and others.

The dominant tendency in Christian and utilitarian thought is to answer these questions in terms of benevolence. It is supposed that the obligation to act for the good of others extends to all human beings and that the best hope of doing so lies in fostering benevolence in moral agents.

My purpose here is to argue that this view is mistaken. Benevolence is not a particularly important virtue, and fostering it to the extent that many, but by no means all, Christians and utilitarians find desirable is fueled by sentimentalism and risks immorality. There is no good reason why we, as moral agents, should be benevolent toward the vast majority of mankind. To insist that nevertheless we should be benevolent is sentimental, because inappropriate feelings are encouraged to take up the slack created by the absence of reasons. Furthermore, this insistence is likely to divert our attention away from our own bailiwick, where the demands of morality are difficult enough to meet, toward imperfectly understood distant situations. Consequently, extending benevolence beyond the limits set by reason jeopardizes the fulfillment of clear obligations in familiar contexts where our

I am indebted to Berel Lang, Bonnie Steinbock, and Eddy Zemach for help with this paper.

responsibility is unquestionable. Undue emphasis on benevolence leads to squandering our moral resources.

Thus, part of my view is that benevolence is merely one virtue among many, on a level perhaps with amiability and punctuality, but its lack is not a serious moral failing, and it may be compensated for by strengthening other aspects of our characters. Benevolence is certainly a pleasing character trait, it carries with it some moral merit, but it is not the moral master-motive, as many Christians and utilitarians suppose. The other part of my view, concerning the inclusiveness of the obligation to act for the good of others, is more equivocal. I doubt that there are good reasons for extending the obligation to all human beings. But I shall not try to substantiate this here. I shall argue for the more modest claim that benevolence does not provide a good reason for doing so.

II

Benevolence is closely related to altruism, kindness, humaneness, compassion, generosity, charity, and love (understood as *agape* or *caritas*). The relevant definition in *The Oxford English Dictionary* is: "Disposition to do good, kindness, generosity, charitable feeling (toward mankind)." "Benevolence" has a general and a specific sense. It may mean the disposition to do good, or the specific forms in which the disposition may manifest itself. Thus, altruism may be understood as benevolence directed toward others, compassion as benevolence shown at someone's suffering, generosity as benevolence issuing in giving people more than they are owed. I shall use "benevolence" in its general sense and ignore the boundaries between its specific senses and the cognates listed above. I shall also ignore the distinction between benevolence and beneficence, the tendency to act for the good of others, since only the most unusual cases of benevolence, if indeed any, fail to issue in action.

Benevolence, then, is a disposition to do good. It is a character trait, in the sense explained by Brandt.[1] But, while many character traits, like having a poor memory, or being loquacious or taciturn, are morally neutral, benevolence is morally desirable. It is a moral excellence, a virtue, because it fosters conformity to one main requirement of morality. However, while some virtues, like courage, conscientiousness, and justice, for instance, are very important to moral life, others, such as being polite, even-tempered, or cheerful, are negligible. It is a crucial question whether benevolence is like the former or the latter. Although the distinction between important and

---

[1] R.B. Brandt, "Traits of Character: A Conceptual Analysis," *American Philosophical Quarterly*, vol. 7 (1970), pp. 23–37.

unimportant virtues cannot be sharply drawn, we may say that, as a rule of thumb, important virtues are normally required by the moral life whatever forms it may take, while many different forms of perfectly moral life are possible without the minor virtues. The tendency of many Christians and utilitarians is to regard benevolence as the most important virtue, while my view is that it is merely a minor one.

Benevolence is composed of emotive, cognitive, and motivational elements. Among these elements, the emotive one is primary and dominant. The fundamental drive of benevolence is the feeling that we care for the good of others; it ranges from rejoicing if others flourish, through many intermediate stages, to being distressed if we witness suffering. The cognitive element guides and corrects the identification of people and situations in whose presence benevolent feelings are appropriate; it aims to resolve conflicts between the dictates of benevolence and those of justice, prudence, selfishness, and so forth; and it exerts critical control over the actions benevolence prompts us to take. This last introduces the motivational element of benevolence. For benevolence is not merely a feeling guided by critical reflection; it is also an active disposition moving us to bring about or enhance the welfare and to reduce or prevent the suffering of others.

Following Shaftesbury, Hutcheson, Butler, and Hume, I regard benevolence as a basic human disposition.[2] To put it in Humean terms: benevolence is a natural virtue, a basic, given element of human nature. "I am of the opinion," writes Hume, "that tho' it be rare to meet one, who loves any single person better than himself; yet 'tis rare to meet with one, in whom all the kind affections, taken together, do not overbalance all the selfish."[3] And if we are tempted to ask why this is so, Hume replies: "It is needless to push our researches so far as to ask, why we have humanity or a fellow-feeling with others. It is sufficient, that this is experienced to be a principle of human nature. . . . No man is absolutely indifferent to the happiness and misery of others. The first has a natural tendency to give pleasure; the second pain. This every one finds in himself."[4] (For contemporary supporting evidence, see Brandt.[5])

[2] On the last three, see T.A. Roberts, *The Concept of Benevolence: Aspects of Eighteenth-Century Moral Philosophy* (London: Macmillan, 1973).
[3] D. Hume, *A Treatise of Human Nature*, ed. L.A. Selby-Bigge (Oxford: Clarendon, 1960), p. 487.
[4] D. Hume, *An Enquiry Concerning the Principles of Morals*, ed. L.A. Selby-Bigge (Oxford: Clarendon, 1961), pp. 219–220.
[5] R.B. Brandt, "The Psychology of Benevolence and Its Implications for Philosophy," *Journal of Philosophy*, vol. 73 (1976), pp. 429–453.

We can sum up the discussion so far by noting that benevolence has the following characteristics:

(1) it is primarily an emotive disposition to care about others' welfare,
(2) it is a morally desirable character trait, hence a virtue,
(3) it has a dominant emotive element, guided by critical reflection and issuing in action, and
(4) it is a basic component of human nature to be found in all normal people.

The conjunction of these characteristics defines what I shall call *limited benevolence*. But there is also *generalized benevolence*.

III

The difference between limited and generalized benevolence is the addition of universality and impartiality. Universality may refer either to the possession or to the object of benevolence. Limited benevolence attributes its possession to all human beings, while generalized benevolence goes beyond universal possession and claims as well that the objects of benevolence are all human beings. This is not a verbal disagreement, but a substantive moral dispute. Champions of generalized benevolence do not hold the obviously false view that all human beings have a disposition to foster the welfare of all human beings. Their view is that, as a matter of fact, all human beings have limited benevolence and, as a matter of morality, they ought also to have universal benevolence. According to them, moral progress consists in expanding limited benevolence until it embraces all human beings. A representative expression of this view is that "the 'general object' of morality. . .is to expand our sympathies, or, better, to reduce the liability to damage inherent in their natural tendency to be narrowly restricted."[6] Those, like myself, who are unwilling to give generalized benevolence pride of place in morality disagree about the moral importance of expanding limited benevolence in the direction of universality.

But the universality of benevolence does not completely express the moral vision of its Christian and utilitarian defenders, for universality is compatible with the unequal distribution of benevolence, provided everyone receives some of it. The moral vision also requires impartial distribution. The relevant Christian text is the second of the two "great commandments" upon which "hang all the law and the prophets": "Thou shalt love thy neighbour as thyself,"[7] which Kierkegaard, writing in one dominant tradition of interpretation, glosses as "Your neighbour is every man. . . . He is your neighbour on the basis of equality with you before God: but this equality absolutely

[6] G.J. Warnock, *The Object of Morality* (London: Methuen, 1971), p. 26.
[7] Matthew, 22:37–40.

every man has, and he has it absolutely."[8] The secular version of this view is expressed by Sidgwick: "Utilitarianism is sometimes said to resolve all virtues into universal and impartial Benevolence:. . .we should aim at Happiness generally as our ultimate end, and so consider the happiness of any one individual as equally important with the happiness of any other."[9]

It is worth noting that neither Christians nor utilitarians need to accept the impartiality requirement of generalized benevolence. Bishop Butler, for instance, is a Christian who does not. He writes: "The love of our neighbour is the same with charity, benevolence, or good-will," and as to the question of "Who is our neighbor?" he replies "that part of mankind, that part of our country, which comes under our immediate notice, acquaintance and influence, and with which we have to do."[10] And somewhat more pungently, Stephen, the most cantankerous of utilitarians, says: "I wish for my own good; I wish for the good of my family and friends; I am interested in my nation; I will do acts of good nature to miscellaneous people come in my way. . . . Show me a definite person doing a definite thing and I will tell you whether he is my friend or my enemy; but as to calling all human creatures indiscriminately my brothers and sisters, I will do no such thing. I have far too much respect for real relations to give these endearing names to all sorts of people whom I know not and for whom, practically speaking, I care nothing at all."[11] But these are minority views. The dominant Christian view is that the neighbors we are enjoined to love include everybody, and our love for them should be impartial;[12] and many utilitarians regard generalized benevolence as the moral master-motive. As Smart puts it: "the utilitarian must appeal to some ultimate attitudes. . . . The sentiment to which he appeals is generalized benevolence, that is, the disposition to seek happiness, or at any rate, in some sense or another, good consequences, for all mankind."[13]

So generalized benevolence has the four characteristics of limited benevolence listed at the end of the previous section, and two additional characteristics:

(5) it is universal, in being directed toward all human beings, and
(6) it is impartial, in being directed toward all human beings equally.

In the rest of the paper, I shall consider two questions: first, is it true that morality requires expanding our limited benevolence toward generalized

---

[8] S. Kierkegaard, *Works of Love*, trans. H. Hong and E. Hong (New York: Harper, 1962), p. 2.
[9] H. Sidgwick, *The Methods of Ethics* (Indianapolis: Hackett, 1981), p. 241.
[10] J. Butler, *Fifteen Sermons* (London: Bell, 1953), pp. 185–187.
[11] J.F. Stephen, *Liberty, Equality, Fraternity* (Cambridge: University Press, 1967), p. 240.
[12] For a contemporary account of the Christian view, see G. Outka, *Agape: An Ethical Analysis* (New Haven: Yale University Press, 1972).
[13] J.J.C. Smart and B. Williams, *Utilitarianism: for and against* (Cambridge: University Press, 1973), p. 7.

benevolence? I shall deny that this is true. The second question is: assuming only limited benevolence, is it true that it is an important, perhaps the most important, virtue? I shall deny this as well.

IV

Let us approach the first question by discussing Hume, the most notable defender of limited benevolence.[14] Hume notes that "it may be affirm'd, that there is no such passion in human minds, as the love of mankind, merely as such, independent of personal qualities, of services, or of relation to ourself."[15] The point is not the trivial one that even generalized benevolence must take concrete forms and have concrete objects. Rather, Hume claims that human nature excludes generalized benevolence: "we perceive, that the generosity of men is very limited, and that it seldom extends beyond their friends and family, or, at most, beyond their native country. Being thus acquainted with the nature of man, we expect not any impossibilities from him; but confine our view to that narrow circle, in which any person moves, in order to form a judgment of his moral character."[16] Christians and utilitarians may go quite some way in agreeing with Hume, for they can accept the fact of limited benevolence and go on to urge changing it, as Mill, for instance, does: "In an improving state of the human mind, the influences are constantly on the increase which tend to generate in each individual a feeling of unity with all the rest; which, if perfect, would make him never think, or desire, any beneficial condition for himself, in the benefits of which they are not included."[17] But Hume's claim is stronger, and it does not allow for this compromise. He thinks that the proposed change from limited to generalized benevolence is both impossible, as we have just seen, and undesirable as well. For "it is wisely ordained by nature, that private connections should commonly prevail over universal views and considerations; otherwise our affections and actions would be dissipated and lost, for want of a proper limited object."[18]

We can construct three arguments, inspired by Hume, for limited and against generalized benevolence. The first is factual: generalized benevolence does not exist. Human nature is so constructed that our benevolence begins with ourselves. It expands outward toward others, but it proportionately weakens as the connection between ourselves and others becomes more

---

[14] I am indebted for my discussion to D. Miller's *Philosophy and Ideology in Hume's Political Thought* (Oxford: Clarendon, 1981); I also draw on my "Civility and Society," *History of Philosophy Quarterly*, vol. I (1984), pp. 429–443.
[15] Hume, *Treatise*, p. 481.
[16] *ibid.*, p. 602.
[17] J.S. Mill, *Utilitarianism* (Indianapolis: Hackett, 1979), p. 32.
[18] Hume, *Enquiry*, p. 229.

and more remote and impersonal. And when it comes to the vast majority of human beings to whom we are not connected by personal love, family ties, shared customs, or forms of life, it peters out completely. It is perfectly natural that this is so. The injunction that we should go against our natural sentiments and try, artificially, to fan our limited benevolence to embrace total strangers of whose lives and circumstances we are largely ignorant, is wildly unrealistic and unrealizable. Christian and utilitarian rhetoric no doubt urges us to do otherwise, but what such urgings really come down to is a misleadingly expressed wish that human nature should be other than what it is. A sound system of morality must respect facts, yet defenders of generalized benevolence quixotically ignore them. Moralists "must take mankind as they find them, and cannot pretend to introduce any violent change in their principles and ways of thinking. . . . [T]he less natural any set of principles are. . .the more difficulty will a legislator meet with in raising and cultivating them."[19]

The second argument is practical. The only effective way of translating into practical terms such benevolence as we have is to restrict it to familiar contexts. The desire to increase the welfare or to diminish the suffering of others is not enough; we must also know how we should go about doing it. And the more remote contexts are, the less we know about them. The reasonable policy dictated by benevolence is to exercise it in contexts where its requirements are clear and to refrain from wasting scarce resources through dubious action based on inadequate knowledge. It is, for instance, less than useless to donate money for the relief of suffering in distant parts of the world if we do not know, as we are likely not to, what causes the undoubted suffering, how the money will be used, and whether there are dependable safeguards against inefficiency, corruption, and stupidity in its distribution. The moral point of these doubts is not merely the disapproval of waste, but also the fact that suffering exists close to home as well. So the choice is not between wasteful generalized benevolence and none at all, but between generalized benevolence which is likely to be wasteful and limited benevolence which has a far better chance of achieving its object.

The third argument is based on moral psychology. Generalized benevolence misdirects our moral attention. The moral life of most people consists in participation in a network of more or less personal relationships. Our obligations are dictated by family ties, personal love, the jobs we have, the roles we play in the various communities and associations to which we belong, and the laws and customs of our country. It is not easy to discharge these obligations. The difficulty is not merely that selfishness, laziness, and

[19] D. Hume, *Essays, Moral, Political and Literary*, ed. T.H. Green and T.H. Gross (London: Longmans, 1898), vol. I, p. 292.

stupidity often lead us to violate moral obligations, but also that the more intimate the relationships are which give rise to the obligations, the more active must our participation in them be. And intimate relationships are far more complex than impersonal ones. It is much easier to be a good citizen than it is to be a good parent or a good spouse. Intimate relationships place moral demands on our sustained attention. Caring for another person requires nearly as much knowledge, understanding, and seriousness as we lavish on ourselves. And, of course, we often fail. Benevolence motivates us to attend more carefully, to try to fail less. But it is limited benevolence which moves us in this way. For it is not a universal and impartial wish for the good of the other that intimacy calls for. On the contrary, it is attention precisely to the individual qualities of the other person that we owe; love is personal and partial; it is not love, if it does not discriminate in favor of its object. The trouble with generalized benevolence is that it directs our attention away from intimacy and toward universality and impartiality. The more successful it is, the less there is left for everyday moral relationships. The more perfectly generalized our benevolence becomes, the less capable we are of cherishing the individuality, the distinctness, the particularity of others which intimacy requires. Since our primary moral obligations are toward those to whom we are intimately connected, generalized benevolence undermines our fulfillment of them.

In the light of these arguments, we can conclude with Mackie that this Humean position is "a welcome corrective to the tendency, in both Christian and utilitarian morality, to set up a quite impracticable ideal of universal benevolence."[20]

However, this defense of limited benevolence is not yet satisfactory, for our benevolence tends to be too limited. Very often, the change from limited to more generalized benevolence is prevented by selfishness and indifference to the suffering of others. Any defense of limited benevolence, therefore, must answer the question of how far morality requires limited benevolence to extend, before it can justifiably ignore the Christian and utilitarian injunction to extend it universally and impartially. Once again, we can look to Hume for help.

The fundamental tenet of Hume's moral philosophy is that morality is based on the human capacity to have feelings of approval and disapproval. If we approve of something, we call it good, because it produces in us a kind of pleasure, and we disapprove of and call bad whatever produces in us a kind of pain. Moral qualities, thus, are not in objects; they are sentiments objects produce in us. These objects are human beings, and the characteristics which produce the sentiments in us are virtues and vices. Virtues and vices

[20] J. Mackie, *Hume's Moral Theory* (London: Routledge, 1980), p. 127.

may be natural and artificial. Natural virtues are inborn, either as actual character traits, or as propensities to develop them; artificial virtues are habits cultivated to help society flourish. The paradigm of natural virtue is benevolence, which, according to Hume, as we have seen, is and ought to be limited. To understand Hume's answer to the question of how far limited benevolence should extend, we have to understand the roles feelings and reason play in benevolence.

The basic idea is that "[h]uman nature being compos'd of two principal parts, which are requisite in all its actions, the affections and understanding; 'tis certain that the blind motions of the former, without the direction of the latter, incapacitate man for society."[21] Essential to understanding Hume's account of the relation between feeling and reason is the recognition that he is making both a positive and a negative claim. The negative claim de-emphasizes the role of reason by stressing the role of feeling and the lack of motivational force of reason: "reason alone can never produce any action or give rise to volition."[22] The positive claim is that reason directs feelings by enabling us to recognize the appropriate objects toward which feelings are reasonably directed, by finding efficient means of enjoying or avoiding these objects, and by acting as a corrective of feelings. The first two activities of reason need not detain us, but the third contains the key to the answer we are looking for.

According to Hume, "nature provides a remedy in the judgment and understanding, for what is irregular and incommodious in the affections."[23] The remedy is "a convention enter'd into by all members of the society. . . . By this means. . .the passions are restrained in their partial and contradictory motions. . . . Instead of departing from our interest, or from that of our nearest friends. . .we cannot better consult both these interests, than by such a convention; because it is by that means we maintain society, which is so necessary to their well-being and subsistence, as well as to our own."[24] This convention is custom, "the great guide of human life. It is that principle which renders our experience useful to us, and makes us expect, for the future, a similar train of events with those which have appeared in the past. Without the influence of custom, we would be entirely ignorant of every matter of fact beyond what is immediately present."[25] Custom has an invariable and a variable aspect. Its invariable aspect includes "principles which are permanent, irresistable, and universal; such as the customary transition from causes to effects. . . . [These principles] are the foundation of all our

[21] Hume, *Treatise*, p. 493.
[22] *ibid.*, p. 413.
[23] *ibid.*, pp. 488–489.
[24] *ibid.*, p. 489.
[25] Hume, *Enquiry*, pp. 44–45.

thought and action."[26] The variable aspect of custom embraces the historically conditioned conventions which may differ from society to society and from period to period within one society.

So Hume's answer to the question of how far limited benevolence should extend is that it should extend as far as custom justifiably prescribes, but no farther. And the prescriptions of custom are justified if they incorporate both the invariable and natural workings of the human mind and the variable conventions which promote the advantage of the society upon which the welfare of its members depends. Reason acts as a corrective in limited benevolence by guiding the emotional and motivational elements to conform to the justified prescriptions of custom.

In my view, this answer is by and large correct, although it requires some improvement in its details. The chief improvement needed concerns the identity of the invariable principles governing the natural workings of the mind. Hume thought that these were the laws of association: causality, resemblance, and contiguity. We know that Hume's associationist psychology, with its atomism, passive view of the mind, and the list of laws inherited from his empiricist predecessors, is untenable. Nevertheless, Hume was surely along the right track in suggesting that, in extending limited benevolence from ourselves and those we love to others, we should be guided by such considerations as our spatial and temporal proximity to its potential beneficiaries, the history of past interactions between us and them, and a sufficient degree of similarity between them and us to judge what would benefit them. The corollary is that the remoter others are from us, the more hostile or threatening our past contacts were, the greater is the gulf between their form of life and ours, the less reasonable it is to extend our limited benevolence to them. And it adds considerable force to the recommendation to thus restrain our promiscuous benevolent impulses that there is plenty of scope and ample need and justification for acting on them in our own context, established well within the limits reason imposes.

So, what Hume is telling us, and what I believe is right, is that we need good reasons to extend our limited benevolence in more generalized directions. Good reasons can sometimes be given and they may justifiably sway us to look beyond the welfare of ourselves and those we love. But in the absence of such reasons, the moral injunction to promote the well-being of others universally and impartially is either a manifestation of sentimentalism or, worse, a potentially immoral policy leading us to neglect actual for spurious obligations.

It may be objected that since the world has become a global village, we do have reason to care about the suffering of strangers, and we always or very

[26] Hume, *Treatise*, p. 225.

often have an obligation to extend our limited benevolence to them. This objection rests on the mistaken assumption that knowledge of the suffering of others creates an obligation to help them. Surely, knowing that Russian soldiers live in jeopardy of life and limb in Afghanistan, or that many criminals have miserable lives and are afraid to enjoy the fruits of their labors, or that tyrants often suffer from the ingratitude of their subjects does not obligate us to do anything to relieve their suffering. It often makes a difference why people suffer. But suppose that our knowledge is of distant but undeserved suffering: children starving, the innocent being tortured, the helpless being exploited. This is clearly evil. Yet there is a lot of evil in the world, our resources are limited, there are often great practical obstacles in the way of help, and suffering closer to home may have a better claim on our moral attention. So not even the knowledge of undeserved suffering creates an automatic obligation to help. Let us say, however, that we know of the undeserved suffering of faraway strangers, we can help them, and there are no overriding claims on our resources. Do we have an obligation to help them then? I shall grant, for the sake of argument, that then we do have such an obligation. But this still does not show that benevolence has anything to do with discharging it. For we may be moved to relieve suffering by justice, decency, or prudence. Therefore, I do not believe that good reasons support a moral requirement to generalize our limited benevolence.

V

Let us now turn to the second question posed at the end of Section III. Is it true that limited benevolence, quite independently of whether or not it should be generalized, is an important moral virtue? We have seen that many Christians and utilitarians give an affirmative answer. I note in passing that, proceeding from quite different premises, Rousseau[27] and Schopenhauer[28] agree with them; and so also do such contemporary writers as Richard Taylor,[29] Beehler,[30] and Blum.[31] Nevertheless, it seems to me that the moral importance of limited benevolence has been exaggerated. The strategy of my argument will be to discuss briefly three quite common types of moral occurrences, stress their importance for any adequate account of morality, and argue that as their importance is recognized, so the importance attributed to limited benevolence must diminish.

Consider, first, the facts of moral blame: A student is expelled for

[27] See J-J. Rousseau, *Emile*, trans. B. Foxley (London: Dent, 1911).
[28] See A. Schopenhauer, *On the Basis of Morality*, trans. E.J. Payne (Indianapolis: Bobbs-Merrill, 1965).
[29] See R. Taylor, *Good and Evil* (New York: Macmillan, 1970), especially Part III.
[30] See R. Beehler, *The Moral Life* (Oxford: Blackwell, 1978).
[31] See L. Blum, *Friendship, Altruism, and Morality* (London: Routledge, 1980).

cheating; a teacher is suspended for exchanging good grades for sexual favors; a politician is shunned for misusing public office for private gain; one competitor is publicly shamed for spreading malicious lies about another; a person is made to feel guilty for habitual tactlessness; readers become indignant at the conduct of historical or fictional characters; an adult, long after the death of his parents, finally admits to anger and resentment at their cruel treatment of him. In all these cases, moral agents react to the wrongdoing of others by blaming them to various degrees.

Blame is an absolutely central moral phenomenon, for it is the appropriate response to the violation of the requirements of morality, however these requirements are understood. Now the immediate point of blame is to register moral disapproval. And if it is directed at normal moral agents, it causes them at least some pain and certainly no joy. At the very least, they have to convince themselves of its inappropriateness, but, more usually, they have to make excuses, admit culpability, or try to make amends. Thus, the immediate point of blame is not benevolent; it is not directed at the good of the person blamed.

It may be said, however, that although the blame is not immediately benevolent, it is, nevertheless, benevolent in the long run. For, presumably, living according to the requirements of morality is good, and the person blamed for violating its requirements will eventually benefit from the painful experience. The suggestion is that blame is partly a prophylactic and partly a pedagogic measure. Now, this suggestion undoubtedly fits some cases of blame, but it does not fit many others. Certainly, blaming dead or fictional people cannot have these objects. Furthermore, very often blame is felt without being expressed, yet it is none the less appropriate and deserved for that. And, then, there are countless cases of what may be called *ex officio* blame, when blame is properly expressed even though its consequences are known to be the opposite of benevolent. Take a teacher who gives an undeserved "A" after a mutually pleasurable sexual encounter with a student. The grade is a kind of lagniappe, not payment for favors extracted. We may even suppose that the encounter is casual, they both forget it, and no one else knows about it. Yet if it comes to the attention of the teacher's superiors, it is nevertheless right and proper to blame the teacher, even though everyone has benefited from the transgression and taking public notice of it will surely spoil the general serendipity.

It would be a mistake to suppose that although blame may not benefit the person blamed even in the long run, it is nevertheless benevolent, because it strengthens the institution of morality which is for the good of everyone. Obviously, blame serves the cause of morality, and it is the truism with which we began that morality is, at least in part, for the good of others. But it does not follow, and it is not true, that the source of individual acts of moral blame must be benevolence. Parents often blame their children out of benevolence. The usual source of moral blame, however, is not paternalistic. We blame wrongdoers out of a sense of justice, or because integrity requires us to express public moral condemnation, or because we want to make it clear to others where we stand, or because we think that wrongdoing ought to be punished. Justice, integrity, and justified resentment exist alongside benevolence as sources of moral blame. And they, rather than benevolence, may be what justifiably leads us to blame others.

The conclusion that follows is that although moral blame may be benevolent, it is very often not. Insofar as moral agents are motivated by limited benevolence, they will be disinclined to engage in nonbenevolent blame. Thus, either limited benevolence must be further limited so as to coexist with this type of nonbenevolent motivation and conduct, or an important part of morality is excluded by the emphasis on limited benevolence.

A second set of facts whose existence must limit the moral importance assigned to limited benevolence concerns meeting one's obligations. There are *prima facie* moral reasons for paying debts, keeping promises, telling the truth, and honoring contracts. Undoubtedly, there are many occasions when meeting our obligations directly involves the welfare of others. The fact that others will suffer because of our lapses may give us added reasons for being dutiful. But their suffering is a reason *added* to the already existing one; the *prima facie* reasons for meeting our obligations hold even if doing so has no immediate effect on anyone's welfare. One should pay debts even to the very rich, keep promises although no one else remembers them, not lie to save general embarrassment, and do one's share regardless of there being no urgent need for it. Of course, there may be excuses for not doing any of these things; but in the normal course of events, morality requires that they be done.

Let us call obligations *onerous* if honoring them is difficult and unpleasant for the agent and if other people do not immediately benefit from the resulting actions. Morality often requires the discharge of onerous obligations, but it is conscientiousness and a sense of duty, rather than benevolence, which motivates moral agents to do so. People moved chiefly by benevolence will be largely indifferent to their onerous obligations; and people who do live up to their onerous obligations cannot be moved chiefly by limited benevolence. So we find, once again, that the moral importance attributed to limited benevolence must be reduced, this time to allow for the claims of onerous obligations.

It may be objected that discharging onerous obligations does not, as a matter of logic, exclude the motivational force of limited benevolence. For moral agents may be moved by limited benevolence not to seek, by direct action, the immediate benefit of others, but to seek their welfare indirectly by aiming at the general welfare in the long run. I think that such motivation is logically possible, and I am willing to concede that some few saintly people may actually be motivated solely by their vision of the remote general welfare. But as a matter of common moral psychology, such simplicity of motivation is extremely rare. Most people's reasons for moral action are a mixture of conscientiousness, justice, a desire to avoid guilt and shame, integrity, the goal of living up to their individual moral ideals, as well as limited benevolence.

The discussion of the facts of moral blame and obligation led to the observation that our moral psychology usually involves many motives in addition to limited benevolence. The implication, in both cases, was that as we recognize the moral importance of nonbenevolent motivation, so we must reduce the moral importance we attribute to limited benevolence. This thought leads directly to the last set of facts to which I want to call attention: the existence and frequency of moral conflicts.

Moral conflicts may occur in different ways. They may be conflicts between the requirements of morality and the requirements of politics, religion, or art; or the conflicts may be between the prescriptions of different moral traditions; or they may be between people with conflicting moral allegiances. The type of moral conflict I want to concentrate on, however, occurs within individuals who are not split between different moral traditions. One form such conflicts may take is having conflicting moral motives: moral agents may be impelled by praiseworthy motives to act in incompatible ways. For instance, limited benevolence may motivate them to show forgiveness and mercy to a wrongdoer, while justice may motivate them to mete out appropriate punishment. Such conflicts are a ubiquitous feature of moral life.

The significance of this kind of conflict, in the present context, is that it cannot be resolved simply by asserting the supremacy of limited benevolence whenever it encounters contrary moral requirements. For the mere fact that other moral requirements frequently conflict with limited benevolence shows that limited benevolence is not the moral master-motive. Now perhaps it ought to be dominant, but that claim requires supporting arguments. If such arguments are available, then they must appeal to some considerations deeper than either limited benevolence or whatever it conflicts with in order to show why limited benevolence should be preferred. But, then, the dominant moral requirement would be set by whatever that deeper consideration turns out to be and not by limited benevolence. If, on the other hand, no argument is given for resolving moral conflicts in favor of limited benevolence, then we can safely ignore the recommendation as moralizing sentimentalism. So the existence of this kind of moral conflict further undermines the attribution of central moral importance to limited benevolence by showing that other moral considerations often take justifiable precedence over limited benevolence.

Another form moral conflicts may take is moral agents being motivated by incompatible moral and nonmoral requirements. The point of noting this is that limited benevolence may appear on both sides of this sort of conflict. It may be a moral motive and conflict, for instance, with self-interest, or it may be a nonmoral motive and move us toward preferring, say, the morally unjustifiable claim of someone we love to the morally justifiable claim of a total stranger. And, of course, nonbenevolent moral considerations may outweigh benevolent nonmoral considerations. But if limited benevolence were the moral master-motive, this could not or should not happen. From the fact that it does happen, we can infer that the claims of limited benevolence are not overriding. In the absence of an argument showing that limited benevolence ought to be overriding, we are justified in concluding that limited benevolence is merely one of several moral virtues, and that morality may well prompt us to ignore its claims for weightier moral claims.

VI

By way of a conclusion, I shall consider an objection defenders of the central moral importance of benevolence may make to my argument. The objection is that in making the case of limited and against generalized benevolence and a case for the limited importance of limited benevolence I constantly appealed to facts. My opponents may concede that the facts tell against the centrality of benevolence as things are and go on to insist that this does not only fail to undermine their claim, but that it also endows it with an even stronger point. For what they are saying, they may explain, is that benevolence ought to have a centrally important role in morality, and this is independent of what role it actually has. Thus, the objection invites us to treat the case for benevolence as a moral recommendation.

Faced with a moral recommendation, we must ask what reason there is for accepting it. Here my opponents give either a noncognitivist or a cognitivist answer. With his usual forthrightness, Smart offers a noncognitivist answer: "a man's ultimate ethical principles depend on his attitudes and feelings. . . . In adopting such a meta-ethics, I do, of course, renounce the attempt to *prove* the act-utilitarian system. I shall be concerned with stating it in a form in which it may appear persuasive to some people, and to show how it may be defended against many objections."[32] My reasons for rejecting this answer are that it is an unpersuasive and indefensible morality which leads to neglecting our obligations in the name of universality and impartiality, as generalized benevolence does, and which is incompatible with the moral

---

[32] Smart and Williams, *Utilitarianism*, pp. 4–5.

importance of blame, obligation, and conflict, as the attribution of central importance to limited benevolence is.

The cognitivist answer encounters a peculiar difficulty in defending benevolence: it must offer reasons for grounding morality on a feeling or an attitude. One would think that the stronger are the adduced reasons, the more they undercut the emotive grounding of morality, while the weaker are the reasons, the more they push cognitivism in the direction of non-cognitivism. But I shall gloss over this difficulty and interpret the cognitivist claim as follows. It is a truth that one chief aim of morality, the good of others, would be best served if limited benevolence were a very important moral motive and if it were generalized in the direction of universality and impartiality. Therefore, those who are committed to the good of others ought to champion benevolence.

My argument against this answer has been to deny the truth of the claim that either limited or generalized benevolence is a particularly important means to the good of others. I have argued that the good of others is served better if we take care to discharge our obligations in our own bailiwick than if we try to relieve suffering in distant and poorly understood contexts. And I have argued further that limited benevolence is only one of several motives which may prompt us to act for the good of others. A sense of duty, justice, decency, personal ideals, prudence, the desire to avoid guilt or shame are some others. Hence, although benevolence is a virtue, it is only a minor one.

To close on a cautionary note: I have not been arguing against Christian or utilitarian morality *per se*, but only insofar as they attribute central moral importance to benevolence; nor have I been arguing against helping strangers, but only against appealing to benevolence to justify the claim that we have an obligation to do so; and I do not think that there is anything wrong with benevolence, but only that the moral claims for it should not be inflated.

Nevertheless, my view is not rendered inconsequential by these qualifications. For it follows from it that the next time we are exhorted to live up to our obligation to relieve misery in distant lands, we may justifiably ask to be supplied with a reason for this supposed obligation.

Philosophy, SUNY at Albany

GENEROSITY AND PROPERTY IN ARISTOTLE'S
POLITICS

By T. H. Irwin

I

Etymology might encourage us to begin a discussion of Aristotle on philanthropy with a discussion of *philanthropia*; and it is instructive to see why this is not quite the right place to look. The Greek term initially refers to a generalized attitude of kindness and consideration for a human being. The gods accuse Prometheus of being a 'human-lover', intending the term in an unfavorable sense, when he confers on human beings the benefits that should have been confined to the gods.[1] Aristotle uses the abstract noun only once, to refer to sympathetic fellow-feeling (*Rhet.* 1390a18–23); and he mentions our feeling of kinship with other human beings to explain our approval of the *philanthropos* person (*Eth. Nic.* 1155a16–21). *Philanthropia* is the attitude of a kind and considerate person, even if she lacks material resources, and it can be displayed without the transfer of material resources.

In later Greek, however, *philanthropia* and its cognates tend to suggest some definite favor done by a superior to an inferior. Philanthropy is the attitude that God displayed towards human beings in the Incarnation (Titus 3.4); and it became a standard virtue of kings, especially of the Roman Emperor. Papyri address the Emperor as "Your Philanthropy," and Julian is referred to as "the most divine, greatest, and most philanthropic king."[2] Any exercise of royal favor, including relief from taxation or some other concession, was recognized as a *philanthropon*; and eventually the term simply refers to a cash payment, suffering the fate that 'gratuity' and 'honorarium' have suffered in English. As one student writes, "Deinde verbum *philanthropia* vel *philanthropon* exarescit, ut ita dicam, in sententiam 'salarii' vel 'mercedis annuae'."[3] Another student remarks that this "'love of man' retained a strong admixture of condescension."[4] The use of the term for the Emperor's

---

[1] See Aeschylus, *Prometheus Vinctus*, 11, 28.
[2] See *Sylloge Inscriptionum Graecarum*, ed. W. Dittenberger, 3rd edition, vol. 2 (Leipzig: S. Hirzel, 1917), no. 906b. For other references, see B. Snell, *The Discovery of the Mind* (Cambridge, MA: Harvard University Press, 1953), pp. 246–252. This is in turn largely based on S. Tromp de Ruiter, "De vocis quae est *philanthropia* significatione atque usu," *Mnemosyne*, vol. 59 (1931–32), pp. 271–306. For "Your Philanthropy" see Tromp de Ruiter, p. 301.
[3] Tromp de Ruiter, "De vocis," p. 293.
[4] Snell, *Discovery*, p. 252, referring to the use of *to philanthropon* for a tip.

exercise of his arbitrary power suggests that his subjects became used to regarding as an act of kindness and charity what they might properly have regarded as a right.

The English term 'philanthropy' seems initially to have been a conscious borrowing of the Greek to express a concept for which, Dryden claimed, there was no exact English term. Bacon speaks appropriately of "The affecting of the Weale of Man: which is that the Graecians call Philanthropie."[5] This very general sense persists in the *OED*'s definition: "Love to mankind; practical benevolence towards men in general; the disposition or active effort to promote the happiness and well-being of one's fellow-men." But probably this definition has not quite caught up with the more restricted modern use of the term for organized "good works" undertaken by private societies. For this sense, the *OED* quotes two interesting nineteenth-century passages. A magazine in 1830 mentions "a convention met for the purpose of philanthropizing the blacks"; and a newspaper expresses some reservations: "Till they get them [votes] we look jealously at these attempts to philanthropize woman *malgré lui*."

On the difference between philanthropy and other forms of benevolence, *Webster's* is more definite than the *OED*. To a definition similar to that in the *OED* it adds a second definition of 'philanthropist': "a generous giver to education, charity, social work, &c; a liberal benefactor." In comparing philanthropy with charity it comments:

> Philanthropy, the broader term, is the spirit of active good will towards one's fellow men, especially as shown in efforts to promote their welfare; charity (cf. mercy) is benevolence as manifested in provision, whether public or private, for the relief of the poor; as, "In benevolence, they excel in *charity*, which alleviates individual suffering, rather than in *philanthropy*, which deals in large masses and is more frequently employed in preventing than in allaying calamity" (Lecky).[6]

In these passages we probably recognize something closer to our most frequent use of 'philanthropy' than is evident in the *OED*'s very general sense.

The fortunes of the cognate Greek and English terms seem quite strikingly similar in some ways, and significantly different in others. Both terms initially refer to a general attitude of good will that could be expressed in many different ways by people in quite different material positions, and later come to refer to a more definite material transaction, frequently (in Greek)

---

[5] These references are taken from *OED*, s.vv.
[6] Quoted from *Webster's New World Dictionary* (New York: Simon & Schuster, 1934).

or normally (in English) involving a benefit by a superior to an inferior. But whereas the Greek term easily and frequently refers to favors conferred by the state, the English term does not. We normally think, for instance, of the welfare state not as an exercise in philanthropy, but as a replacement of it.

This excursion into lexicography will perhaps introduce us to some of the reasons for doubt about the value of philanthropy, as presently understood. In both Greek and English a term initially referring to an uncontroversially desirable attitude to human beings comes to be used to put a good face on the largesse of the better-off to the worse-off. It is easy to suppose that we leave room for philanthropy only by slighting the claims of justice. Philanthropy requires the philanthropic person (or institution) to have some surplus beyond her needs, and requires a beneficiary who is in some way significantly worse off than the benefactor. It is natural to ask whether the inequality between benefactor and beneficiary could not have been removed by some other means, and whether the interests of the beneficiary could not be better served by making him less dependent on the charitable impulses of the benefactor. This is the sort of suspicion that Kant expresses in his rather pointed "casuistical questions" about beneficence:

> The ability to practice beneficence, which depends on property, follows largely from the injustice of the government, which favours certain men and so introduces an inequality of wealth that makes others need help. This being the case, does the rich man's help to the needy, on which he so readily prides himself as something meritorious, really deserve to be called beneficence at all?[7]

Kant points out that private property and inequality leave room for philanthropy; if they must be assumed, then philanthropy is better than no philanthropy, but we might wonder if it would not be better to remove the conditions that make philanthropy desirable.

A natural reply to Kant's suspicion is to defend the system of private property and the inequalities that it may permit. One familiar defense is historical and deontological, appealing to the right of acquisition, and the resulting justice of property holdings that are licensed by this right. If we accept such a defense, and if we believe that the right of acquisition overrides other moral principles, we can freely admit that everyone would be better off under a more redistributive system. We will simply argue that such consequences cannot outweigh the claims of justice, even if justice has regrettable consequences.

A different and equally familiar line of defense might argue for private

---

[7] Immanuel Kant, *The Doctrine of Virtue*, trans. M.J. Gregor (New York: Harper and Row, 1964), p. 122 (Akad., p. 453).

property on utilitarian grounds, claiming that it promotes the relevant good consequences better than any alternative system would, and that these good consequences outweigh any bad side effects of the sort that Kant alludes to. This consequentialist defense leaves us with two possible attitudes toward private philanthropy and beneficence. We might admit that on the whole its existence is regrettable, but unavoidable, as an unfortunate side effect of desirable arrangements of property. Alternatively, we might argue that in fact it is more efficient than any other system, and in fact is one of the arrangements that positively promotes the good consequences of private property.

It is worth sketching these different and familiar strategies so that we can see what is distinctive about Aristotle's view of beneficence and private generosity. He does not offer a deontological defense, appealing simply to a basic principle about the justice of private property.[8] Nor, however, does he exactly offer either of the consequentialist defenses I mentioned. He certainly does not think the opportunity for private beneficence is a regrettable side effect of the beneficial arrangement of private property. Nor does he think its value is merely instrumental, lying in any contribution to the further consequences resulting from private property. Indeed, he practically reverses this order of argument; he actually defends private property because it provides the resources for the exercise of beneficence, and he regards the exercise of beneficence as valuable in itself. He does not have to prove that beneficence is more efficient in distributing goods than any alternative method would be; indeed, he can readily allow some inefficiency as a fair price to pay for the good of exercising beneficence.

Beneficent activity needs to be very good if it is to play the role Aristotle intends for it.[9] If we are to examine his defense of generosity, we need to see first what is so good about it, and then why it requires private property.

II

Aristotle develops his views on generosity and property most fully in his criticism of Plato's *Republic*. Plato abolishes private property, citing its bad

---

[8] 'Simply' and 'basic' are important here. Aristotle certainly believes the holding of private property is just. On some issues that I treat very briefly here I have benefited from reading Fred Miller's "Aristotle on Property Rights," presented to the Society for Ancient Greek Philosophy, March 1986.

[9] Aristotle's argument from generosity arouses skepticism in L.C. Becker, *Property Rights* (London: Methuen, 1977), p. 86. "But turning remarks like these into a sound argument for property rights is a difficult task. It is difficult because the argument will depend on contestable premises about what counts as an element of virtuous character, as well as contestable premises about human behavior." It is hard to find any argument for property, however, that does not rest on some contestable premises; this fact about Aristotle's argument is hardly a reason for dismissing it. Becker's more specific criticisms are much more reasonable; they are similar (though presented without much argument) to those I offer later.

effects on the unity and harmony of the state, and therefore on the common interest of the citizens.[10] Aristotle argues that Plato's reform will do more harm than good. He points out that without private property citizens have no private resources they can use in generous actions; they are deprived of any initiative that is independent of the coercive authority of the state. The arrangement Aristotle prefers is private ownership and common use, relying on the generosity of individual owners. He defends his preference against Plato as follows:

> Indeed such arrangements are already present in sketchy form in some cities, on the assumption that they are not impossible, and especially in the cities that are finely governed some of them exist and some might easily exist; a person has his own private possessions of which he makes some available for his friends' use and keeps some for his private use. In Sparta, for instance, they have practically common use of each other's slaves, and also of dogs and horses and of the fields in the country, if they need provisions on a journey. Evidently, then, it is better for the possessions to be private but to make them common by the way they are used; and it is the special task of the legislator to see that people of the right sort to do this develop. (1) Further, counting something as our private property enormously increases our pleasure. For one's love towards oneself is certainly not pointless, but is a natural tendency. Certainly, selfishness is justifiably criticized; but selfishness is not loving oneself, but loving oneself more than is right – just as greed [is not love of money, but love of it more than is right], since practically everyone has some love of such things. (2) Moreover, doing favours or giving aid to one's friends or guests (*xenoi*) or companions is most pleasant; and one can do this if possession is private. None of these things, then, results for those who make the city excessively unified. (3) And besides they evidently abolish any function for two of the virtues – for temperance (since it is a fine action to leave a woman alone because of temperance when she belongs to someone else), and for generosity with possessions; for no one's generosity will be evident and no one will do any generous action, since the function of generosity is in the use of possessions. (*Politics* 1263a30–b14)[11]

---

[10] Plato actually abolishes private property and the nuclear family only for the guardian class. I will not keep mentioning this restriction.

[11] In 1263a35–6 I follow H. Richards in reversing the manuscript order of *koinois* and *idois*. His suggestion is mentioned, but not endorsed, in the apparatus of W.D. Ross's text (Oxford: Clarendon Press, 1957).

While Plato's proposal appears to remove the evils resulting from private property, Aristotle believes it is the wrong diagnosis and the wrong cure:

> This sort of legislation might seem appealing and philanthropic. For on hearing it, one accepts it with pleasure, supposing that there will be some remarkable degree of friendship to all. This is especially true when someone condemns the prevailing evils in political systems as the result of not having common property – e.g. legal actions about contracts, judgments about false testimony, and flattery of the rich. None of these, however, is the result of not having common property, but they are the result of vice. For in fact we see that those who have acquired and hold possessions in common actually have far more disputes with each other than those with separate property have. . . . Further, it is only fair to mention not only the evils that they will be rid of by common property, but also the goods they will be deprived of. And in fact their life appears to be altogether impossible. (1263b15–29)

Aristotle argues that the bad results of private property can be removed without removing private property, whereas its good results cannot be secured without private property. Hence Plato offers us a bad bargain. In his own ideal state Aristotle retains private property, but prescribes the common use that allows the benefits of common ownership without abolishing private property (1329b41–1330a2).

A major benefit of private property is the opportunity it provides for generosity; for Aristotle claims that generosity has its function (*ergon*) in the use of possessions (1263b13–14). But here we need to define the questions more sharply. The Aristotelian virtue that encourages beneficent and (in the modern sense) philanthropic activity is generosity, *eleutheriotes* (discussed fully in *EN* iv 1). This plainly involves the transfer of material resources in circumstances where no principle of justice requires it. Without this transfer there is no generous action; and to this extent Aristotle is clearly right to say that generosity has its function in the use of possessions. But Aristotle needs a stronger claim. For in defending private property as a means to generosity, he evidently needs to appeal to a virtue that essentially involves the use of *private* possessions, which are not mentioned in his claim about the function of generosity.

He can show what he needs in either of two ways. First, he might argue that generosity itself requires private property to be generous with. Alternatively, he can concede that generosity is possible without private property, but argue that there is a type of generosity (which we may call "private generosity") that does require private property, and that something of distinctive value is lost if we cannot exercise this virtue. If we are to focus on the most controversial aspects of Aristotle's position, we must see if either of these lines of argument is at all promising. If generosity is possible without private property, one of Aristotle's main arguments for private property collapses. If, however, we confine ourselves to the sort of generosity which is essentially generosity with one's own private property, we can ask Aristotle why this particular sort of generosity is important enough to deserve to be protected by the existence of private property. My discussion of Aristotle's views does not sharply separate his views about property from his views about generosity. I hope this fusing of the two questions will not matter; in the end it should be fairly clear what we have found about each issue.

III

Aristotle's defense of private property reflects one essential aspect of justice in the ideal state. Justice is intended to promote the common interest of members of a community (*EN* 1129b17–19), and the branch of it called "special" justice (1130a14–b5) is meant especially to protect their self-confined interests – those interests that essentially involve the satisfaction of desires for states of oneself rather than states of other people. Such protection will ensure that the state does not impose an unreasonable degree of sacrifice on an individual for the benefit of other members of the community. Since the virtuous person's good consists in more than his purely self-confined goods, justice need not assure him a higher level of self-confined goods than he could achieve under any other arrangement; he will legitimately accept some sacrifice for the sake of the common good that is also part of his own good. However, he will not accept the neglect of his self-confined interest beyond the point where his own interest justifies it. He is not simply a natural resource for promoting other people's interest; that is the status of a slave.

Aristotle uses these points about self-sacrifice to criticize Plato for going to self-defeating extremes in his efforts to make the whole city promote its common interest. Aristotle supposes (most dubiously) that Plato has deprived the guardians of happiness to secure the happiness of the whole city, and argues against Plato that the happiness of the whole cannot be secured by forcing one large part to renounce its own self-confined interest for the sake of the other parts (1264b15–25).

The treatment of the guardians is one sign of Plato's neglect of the self-confined aspects of a person's interest. Aristotle sees the same neglect in his arrangements for property in the ideal city. After alleging inconsistencies in Plato's arrangements he explains, in the passage I quoted earlier, how Plato's abolition of private property also abolishes the valuable activities for which private property is a prerequisite. Plato hopes to strengthen friendship and cooperation in the ideal state; but he has abolished one of the conditions that make friendship valuable. Friendship essentially involves individuals, each of whom is aware of himself as a bearer of distinct self-confined interests, which he freely and willingly adapts to those of the others. With no self-confined interests we have nothing to adapt and nothing to adapt to; and private property strengthens the proper sense of self-confined interest. We do not make friendship and cooperation easier by removing each person's self-confined interest; we deprive friendship and cooperation of their point. The friendship that is supposed to exist in Plato's ideal city will in fact be "watery" (1262b15) because it is supposed to rest on some generalized concern for the common good among people who will lack a sufficiently lively sense of their own self-confined good (1262b7–24).

Aristotle presents a related general criticism of Plato's ideal in attacking what he takes to be the excessively unifying tendencies of Plato's city. Plato recognizes the dangers resulting from different individuals with different conceptions of their self-confined interests; seeing that these conceptions may result in conflict, he thinks it better to remove the difference between people's different conceptions, and to concentrate everyone's individual conception on goals that are shared with everyone else and aim at the common welfare. In Plato's preferred order no one has any conception of a self-confined interest, but everyone devotes her effort to some common good. This is the arrangement that Aristotle rejects as excessive unification. He suggests that Plato treats the individuals as parts of a single organism (cf. 1261a10–22); in failing to recognize their distinct self-confined interests Plato ignores an essential condition for the achievement of their good.[12]

IV

The criticism of Plato's ideal, from the point of view of special justice, assumes that a person's self-confined interest is an important, even an indispensable, part of her good. To see why Aristotle believes this we must refer to his views on freedom and individual initiative.

We can best understand these views by noticing the importance he attributes to leisure, *schole*, in the best life.[13] It is contrasted with being occupied in the production of necessities (1333a30–6); the self-sufficient

---

[12] Aristotle's views on distinctness and unity in political contexts are favorably regarded by M.C. Nussbaum, "Shame, Separateness, and Political Unity," A.O. Rorty, ed., *Essays on Aristotle's Ethics* (Berkeley and Los Angeles: University of California Press, 1980), chap. 21. I do not discuss Artistotle's own use of the organic analogy in 1253a15–29, 1337a27–30; there is an apparent prima facie difficulty in making it consistent with his criticism of Plato's use of the analogy.

[13] On leisure, see 1326b26–32, 1333a30–b5, 1334a2–40, 1337b28–32; cf. 1269a34–6, 1273a24–5, 1329a1–2, 1341a28. Leisure is not 'being at leisure', where that suggests being unoccupied; nor is it recreation as opposed to serious business (cf. *EN* 1176b27–1177a6).

city has to provide enough resources for a life of leisure, which is not occupied in securing the necessary resources (1326b26–32).

Leisure matters to Aristotle because it extends the scope of a person's choice. In necessary occupations my choice is limited; I have to do something to make a living, and I have to conform to the demands of my occupation if it is the source of my living.[14] A rational agent who chooses effective rational agency in the whole of his life will want to make as many choices as possible in conditions of leisure. Hence we will be best off in a community in which our characters and decisions have maximum effect.

Leisure, as Aristotle construes it, is a means to allow individual initiative and control in political action. By advocating leisure as a means, he shows that he values individual initiative and control as an end. Since he values these, we can see why he values the exercise of generosity to which private property is supposed to be a means.

If I have my own supply of external goods under my own control, it is my choice and decision that determines what happens to it. If I do not control it, I must depend on someone else; nothing is under my control to use in generous actions. Even if the result of private generosity is the very same as the result that the wise legislator would prescribe, the fact that it results from the private generosity of many is a further good feature of it that is lost if the result is produced by legislation. The importance of external goods for individual initiative explains why special justice is needed. It is needed not simply to assure to everyone the external goods he needs, but also to assure him of the goods he needs to support the initiatives he takes. This is why Aristotle will not think the demands of justice are satisfied if everyone simply gets what he needs.

Aristotle, therefore, does not defend private generosity primarily by appeal to efficiency. He criticizes Plato's arrangement as an ideal, and offers his own as an alternative ideal, not simply as the best practical option in empirically likely circumstances. He criticizes Plato for making private generosity impossible, because he thinks Plato's arrangement betrays failure to recognize the importance and value of individual initiative in a person's good. Aristotle values private generosity, and therefore the private property that allows it, because it expresses the virtuous person's desire to benefit others through his own choice and the exercise of his own initiative.

---

[14] Though my choices and decisions are important, they make less difference, and are less free, than they are when I am not constrained by the demands of necessity; under these constraints the difference between the virtuous and the vicious decision is less clear. (On necessity and voluntary action, see *EN* 1110a11–19, 1115b7–10, 1116a29–b3.) The virtuous person will act virtuously as far as he can; but his virtuous decision will not have the same opportunity to design his life that it will have when he has leisure. If the necessities of life do not constrain me to do just or temperate action (cf. 1318b13–14), then it is entirely a matter for my decision, and the shape of my life will depend on my decision.

We now seem to have a preliminary answer to our question about why *private* generosity is so important to Aristotle. He believes that if virtuous activity is to express my initiative (as opposed to my conformity to the law), it must use resources that are entirely up to me to use; they must be wholly at my disposal, and hence they must be my private property.

V

To avoid misinterpretation of Aristotle's defense of private property and generosity, we should notice its significantly restricted scope. Private property is meant for a state in which all the citizens are in a position to live a life of leisure and virtue, so that each has a sufficient supply of externals to free him from concern with them. Aristotle is not arguing for private charity to the destitute and desperately poor; indeed he argues against this in stressing the evil of letting the lower classes be impoverished and dependent (e.g., 1309a20–6). In describing land tenure in the ideal city Aristotle first reaffirms the principle of private property with friendly provision for sharing (1329b41–1330a2). But he at once makes a crucial exception to the general rule of private property, seeing that "none of the citizens must lack sustenance" (1330a3); the ideal city subordinates the protection of private property to the avoidance of great inequalities of wealth and poverty. It follows the Spartan custom of common meals (*sussitia*), but rejects the Spartan method of administering them. A Spartiate who became too poor to pay his contribution to the common meals had to relinquish his status as a full citizen (1271a26–37, 1272a12–21). Instead of allowing this increasing inequality, Aristotle prefers the Cretan system that requires public provision for the common meals, and he designates publicly-owned land for this purpose (1330a3–13).

This provision for collective ownership of land in the ideal state should be an important corrective to a one-sided view of Aristotle's criticism of Plato on private property, since it shows very clearly which principles Aristotle takes to be prior to which others. All the disadvantages of public ownership that he urges against Plato are no less present for Aristotle's own arrangement. We could imagine him arguing that the collective farms will be worked with less enthusiasm, and so less productively, than the private land will be, and that in any case we should leave it to the generosity of the richer citizens to make sure that the "truly needy" do not sink into destitution. We might even expect him to challenge the admittedly democratic institution of the common meals, as a restriction on the individual's use of his own resources.[15]

---

[15] See 1265b40–1, where the common meals are said to be a democratic feature of the Spartan system. At 1330a4–5 Aristotle says he will explain later why he favors common meals, but he does not keep his promise anywhere in the extant *Politics*. Presumably the remark in

In fact, he considers none of these objections; and if he had considered them, he could fairly argue that they are subordinate to the overriding demand of securing the necessary means of a good life to all the citizens. Though Aristotle does not say much about the reasons for this subordination, he clearly accepts some restriction on the opportunities to acquire and use property, in order to assure the provision of an important good for the worse-off. It is well worth exploring his grounds for this choice, but I will explore them no further now.

I have called attention to the extent of public ownership advocated by Aristotle, in order to show how circumscribed his defense of private property and generosity actually is, in comparison with some that we are used to. The sort of generosity he wants to protect is more like my lending you my lawn mower and your lending me your hedge cutter, when both of us are in roughly equal conditions and neither depends on the favor of the other. Since these are Aristotle's assumed background conditions for private property, he lays himself open, as he should, to the argument that in conditions where private property encourages poverty, pauperism, clientship, dependence, and social conflict, its advantages may be overridden by the greater importance of avoiding these other evils.

VI

We may be initially sympathetic to Aristotle's defense of private property because it appeals to one highly plausible principle. Aristotle recognizes something important that Plato never clearly recognizes about the relation of an individual to political authority. He sees that my having some initiative and control over what happens to me is a good in itself; he therefore sees that mere efficiency in achieving my other interests is not the only proper standard for the criticism of a political system.

On the other hand, Aristotle acknowledges Plato's charge that private property is to be avoided because it encourages the natural tendency to greed, cupidity, and competitiveness (1263b15–22); for Plato, the abolition of private property is a small price to pay for the removal of these tendencies. Aristotle argues that the blame for these bad results should be placed on vice, not on private property. He thinks it naive to suppose that social conflicts can be removed by altering the distribution of property. He is no less scathing about equalization of property than about the more radical

---

1330a2 about avoiding destitution gives at least part of his reason. Newman notices that Aristotle has quite a bit to explain: "Aristotle, we note, though he is strongly in favour of the household, is also strongly in favour of syssitia or public meal-tables, perhaps a somewhat antagonistic institution." W.L. Newman, ed., *The Politics of Aristotle* (Oxford: Clarendon Press, 1887–1902), vol. 1, p. 333. The same could be said about the public provision for common means in relation to private property.

Platonic solution (1266b38–1267a2). His criticism does not always distinguish necessary from sufficient conditions. He agrees that equality of property is somewhat useful, though not very significant, in preventing conflicts (1267a37–9), and we might agree that it is insufficient without agreeing that it is unnecessary. He evidently believes, however, that private property may be harmless, and that its potential harms can be avoided by the proper sort of moral education.

Aristotle recognizes a reciprocal relation between the characters of citizens and the nature of the political system (1337a11–27). Different conceptions of happiness and of conditions for sharing in it result in different conditions for citizenship, and hence in different political systems (1328a27–b2). A system must preserve itself by forming the right sorts of characters; otherwise the system will find it hard to survive (1292b1–21, 1319b1–4). Moreover, Aristotle argues, conscious planning will make a difference; for some cities allow their unconscious formation of characters to threaten the foundations of the system, and this is what we should expect when they are founded on a partly false conception of happiness. A system that extends its inherent defects into defective characters in its citizens will threaten its own stability; hence the one-sided pursuit of the conception of happiness that underlies an oligarchy or a democracy will eventually threaten the oligarchic or democratic system itself (1310a12–38). The best political system relies on the right conception of happiness, and so educates its citizens in genuine virtues, which in turn support the best political system.

Aristotle believes, then, that the best political system need not forgo the benefits of private property in order to avoid the evils that it may produce in non-ideal states. For the right sort of moral education will produce concern for the genuine virtues and for the common good; a citizen will not prize the accumulation of external goods over the just requirements of his friends or the community, and so he will avoid dangerous competition, flattery, and greed. The institutions of the ideal state and the practices it encourages should support each other, and should not create the sorts of conflicts that undermine the structure of the state. These conflicts would result if moral education encouraged altruism but we were taught to value private property for its advantages to us in competition with others. However, Aristotle intends moral education to teach us the proper use of private property; it is regulated by friendship and justice, and in turn supports the activities appropriate to these virtues. In these conditions private property will actually promote concern for the common interest; it will provide resources for the virtue of generosity without creating serious temptations to vice.

In his support Aristotle might fairly point out that Plato expects profound effects from moral education in his ideal state; it might well seem arbitrary of

Plato to suppose that moral education could not produce the right attitude to private property.

VII

If, however, we are inclined to support Aristotle's appeal to moral education in reply to Plato's attack on private property, it is only fair to notice that a similar argument will support a Platonic rejoinder. For Aristotle argues that the abolition of private property goes against the grain of human nature, violating the natural human pleasure in our own possessions (1263a40–b7), and that the sort of friendship Plato wants to create will be watery, compared with what we are used to in smaller associations. Plato seems free to use Aristotle's own argument in defense of private property, and to insist that the evils that Aristotle mentions will be removed by the right sort of moral education.

Aristotle might argue that Plato overestimates the power of moral education if he thinks it can alter such basic tendencies in human nature. But this is a dangerous line for him to take, since it seems to work equally well against his own appeal to moral education in support of private property. To see how serious an objection this might be, it is worth exploring its implications a little further.

If we are skeptical about Aristotle's appeal to moral education, we may think he puts too little weight on the effects of actual concern with private property. Aristotle would think it was silly to expect moral education to train us to copulate without sexual desire. Is it not equally silly to expect that it will train us to handle private property without the greed, competitiveness, and hostility to others that are normally associated with it? Perhaps these attitudes must be cultivated for the successful accumulation and protection of private property; and once we acquire and cultivate them, Aristotle himself will tell us that it is folly to pretend we can talk ourselves out of deeply ingrained habits. He seems to recognize some aspects of this tension when he allows that generous people may be worse than others at managing their assets (1120b4–6, 14–20), and that the process of acquisition tends to make people more acquisitive and less generous (1120b11–14). Surely he allows too little for the motives that are encouraged by the objective nature of accumulation and possession.

We can strengthen this objection by appealing to one of Aristotle's own arguments. He prohibits the citizens of his ideal state from menial work, because such work is inconsistent with the virtue that is required for a happy life (1328b39–1329a2).[16] In his view, someone who must spend most of his

---

[16] On menial occupations see 1258b37–9, 1337b8–10, 1278a12, 17, 21, 1296b29, 1317a25, 1319a27, 1341b13, 1342a20, 22.

time and effort working for a precarious living, or in dependence on the favor of another, will never develop the right virtues of character for a citizen. If Aristotle is right about this, he has a good prima facie reason for excluding menial workers from citizenship.

This argument seems to assume, however, that the menial occupation itself ruins a person's character, and that it is futile to expect moral education to have any countervailing effect.[17] Aristotle might correctly warn us that moral character cannot simply be imposed on occupations and circumstances. We cannot reasonably exhort someone to care about virtue and force him to spend all his time in occupations where success requires the subordination of virtue to other aims. To expect such results from moral education is to expect too much from it; it is not a magical protection against the influence of other objective circumstances.

If we absorb this salutary reminder, we might be tempted to agree with Aristotle that Plato expects too much in expecting to avoid the bad effects of common ownership by moral education. But how can we then also agree with Aristotle in discounting the bad effects of private property and hoping to avoid them by moral education? It is hard to see what would justify different conclusions in the two cases.

VIII

On this issue the argument seems to have reached a deadlock. Perhaps the deadlock can be resolved by further examination of the nature of moral education and the tendencies it is supposed to mold and modify. At this stage, however, it is useful to examine a further issue of principle.

Aristotle will have a strong point against Plato if he can show that private property involves a distinctive value that will be lost if it is abolished. This notion of distinctive value is quite vague, but quite important to Aristotle. An aggressive person who enjoys throwing his weight around by bullying other people gains some sort of pleasure from this; but Aristotle will not agree that a virtuous person really loses any benefit by forgoing this sort of pleasure in a virtuous life; the loss of the aggressive person's pleasure is not a minus to be offset by the pluses of the virtuous life. Presumably Aristotle will argue that the aggressive person's pleasure is an instance of a species of worthwhile pleasure – say, in the awareness of the exercise of one's own ability – that is also present in the virtuous person's life. Insofar as the aggressive person takes particular pleasure in harming someone else, that pleasure is shameful and dangerous, and it is no loss to him if he is denied it. On the other hand, Aristotle wants to say that the pleasure of sexual intercourse is not replace-

---

[17] It is not clear that Aristotle always takes this view. See 1277b3–7, 1333a6–16, 1337b17–21, 1341b10–17, *Rhet.* 1419b7–9.

able with some nonsexual pleasure; it must itself be a part of the complete virtuous and happy life. In these examples sexual pleasure expresses a distinctive value, and aggressive pleasure does not. It is a difficult matter to discover and evaluate Aristotle's principles, or any reasonable principles, for assigning distinctive value to activities and states; but we can at least say that Aristotle needs to do this at least in a rough and intuitive way.

The question to raise for his criticism of Plato, then, should be whether private generosity expresses some distinctive value. Aristotle's remarks about the pleasure we take in what is our own suggest that he thinks it does; but a plausible argument can be given from Aristotelian premises to show that it does not.

We have seen from Aristotle's defense of leisure that he values freedom and individual initiative. But he does not accept the democratic conception of freedom as 'living as one wishes'.[18] He thinks the democratic conception of freedom is unworthy, because a life that is guided by the political system should not be regarded as slavery, but as safety (1310a36–8). Aristotle concedes that it is slavish to live for another, so that one's actions are determined by the other's will independently of one's own. But he recognizes a crucial exception. The magnanimous person will refuse to live for another, except for a friend (1124b31–1125a2); and actions that would otherwise be menial are not menial if I do them for myself or for a friend (1277b5–7, 1337b17–21). Similarly, the virtuous person's relation to his city is not slavish. If he regards his fellow citizens as his friends, he is concerned about the common good of all of them as a part of his own good. Insofar as his actions are regulated by the common good he is not being made to live for another as the slave is; for the slave's interests have either no weight at all or a weight that is firmly subordinate to the weight of the master's interests, and none of this is true of the citizen.

If this is all true, it seems possible for a citizen in an ideal state to exercise generosity without exclusive ownership. My own generosity may be properly expressed through my role in collective actions; it does not seem to need resources under my exclusive control. Even if we think the practice of generosity requires me to be free to dispose of some resources on my own initiative, it does not follow that the resources must be under my exclusive control. The state might loan them to me, and allow me to dispose of them as I please within certain limits and in certain circumstances; such an arrangement would leave ample room for the exercise of generosity.

We might argue that this is not real generosity, if the virtuous person's action does not cost *him* anything, and that it does not cost him anything unless he gives from his exclusive possessions. But this objection seems to

[18] See 1317a40–b17; cf. 1259a39, 1307a34, 1310a28–36, 1318b39, 1319b30, *Rhet.* 1366a4.

overlook the virtuous person's attachment to the common good. He will regard the distribution of his friend's resources as a cost to himself, because he regards his friend's resources as his own; and he will take the same view of the community's resources. We might object that such identification of one's own interest with the interests of others is impossible or undesirable; but Aristotle should not be easily persuaded by any such objection, since it would undermine his whole account of friendship. Perfectly genuine generosity seems to be quite possible without private property; and to this extent private property seems unnecessary for anything of distinctive value.

Aristotle might perhaps reply that private generosity does express some distinctive value that is overlooked in the account of generosity that we have given. He suggests that self-love naturally attaches itself to something that is exclusively my own, and that without ownership the desirable aspects of self-love will be lost. Once again we may wonder if he is not being pessimistic about the powers of moral education when it suits him.

It may well be important that an individual should have a strongly developed conception of himself as an individual, a source of desires, interests, and claims, distinct from those of other individuals. Exclusive ownership may be one way to develop and strengthen such a conception. But it is hard to see why it should be the only way in Aristotle's ideal state. In a political system where the citizen's interests, views, and advice count in the collective actions of the community, self-love will be appropriately encouraged; it does not seem to need the extra encouragement derived from exclusive ownership. Aristotle has not shown that private property contributes uniquely or distinctively to the exercise of any virtue that we legitimately value; and he has not shown that the sort of generosity that requires private property at my exclusive disposal is a genuine virtue in its own right.

I conclude that Aristotle has not succeeded in the task we imposed on him, of defending essentially private generosity, and therefore the private property that makes it possible. He charges that Plato's system has only the appearance of *philanthropia*; but I do not think he has shown that proper *philanthropia* clearly requires private philanthropy.

IX

We have been discussing Aristotle's advocacy of private property and private generosity as an ideal, and therefore have legitimately compared them with his other ideals, and especially with some other aspects of his ideal state; for present purposes it is irrelevant to object that the other features of the ideal state are impractical.[19] On Aristotle's own terms I think we have

---

[19] It is also hard to say how far Aristotle has a plausible defense for private property in non-ideal states (though he clearly accepts it).

reason to conclude that his defense of private property is seriously defective. It rests on legitimate demands for individual freedom and initiative; but other aspects of the ideal state show that these legitimate demands can be satisfied without private property. Moreover, the rest of Aristotle's theory should warn us of certain dangers in the acceptance of private property, to be measured against its advantages.

Once we see that the ideals safeguarded by private property can be safeguarded in other ways, the advantages secured by private property are fairly small, and we can fairly doubt if they compensate for the dangers. I have not been criticizing Aristotle by appeal to principles foreign to him. I have challenged his defense of private property by appeal to the more general principles of his own political theory.

If I am right, then we had better not look to Aristotle's political theory as a whole for a defense of private property and the private philanthropy that involves the use of private property. I do not want to say that we must at once be skeptical about the defense of private property; before we drew that conclusion we would need to be sure that Aristotle has exhausted all the possible ideals and principles that might be invoked. Still, I think we might reasonably draw some tentative conclusions that go beyond the evaluation of Aristotle's arguments.

(1) It is worth repeating a point I mentioned earlier, that Aristotle defends private initiative in a comparatively small area; he does not accept it as an alternative to state action in the relief of poverty and the provision of basic welfare. To this extent his conception of the proper scope of generosity is far narrower than a Victorian, pre-welfare-state conception of the scope of philanthropy; and anyone who wants to make the Victorian conception into a post-welfare-state conception of philanthropy should take no comfort from Aristotle's arguments.

(2) Though Aristotle could not anticipate the variety of arguments for private property and philanthropy that later theorists have devised, I think he has in fact identified the main ideals that might seem to support private property. If so, then his failure to defend private property successfully from any of these ideals casts some significant doubt on whether a successful defense can be found. As I have said, it remains possible that we could defend private property and generosity as the best expedient in certain empirical circumstances; but in that case we would of course have to weigh its benefits against the costs that Plato emphasizes and Aristotle illegitimately discounts. Many defenders of private property think it is more than a practical expedient, and they ought to be worried by the failure of Aristotle's arguments.

(3) Some defenders of private property may not be worried by Aristotle's failure because they rely on a deontological argument for a right to private

property, and Aristotle does not rely on any such argument. It would be a long story to say what difference this particular appeal to rights ought to make. But I would like to raise one doubt about whether it will really make a basic difference. If someone is prepared to argue that we have a right to private property, he will be well advised to appeal to some further principle about the value of individual freedom and initiative as the basis of this right. Such an appeal takes us straight back to one of the Aristotelian ideals. If my objections to Aristotle are right, an appeal to these ideals is unlikely to show precisely that we have a right to private property. Though Aristotle himself does not explicitly appeal to rights, the weaknesses in his argument allow us to predict weaknesses in arguments appealing to rights.

Philosophy, Cornell University

PRIVATE PHILANTHROPY AND POSITIVE RIGHTS

By Alan Gewirth

How can anyone be opposed to private philanthropy? Such philanthropy consists in persons freely giving of their wealth or other goods to benefit individuals and groups they consider worthy of support. As private persons, they act apart from – although not, of course, in contravention of – the political apparatus of the state. In acting in this beneficent way, the phil-anthropists are indeed, as their name etymologically implies, lovers of humanity; and their efforts are also justified as exercises of their right to freedom, including the free use of the resources they own, which they have presumably acquired by their own free efforts or by the efforts of other persons who have freely transferred these resources to them. Thus, private philanthropy combines two of the highest values of individual and social morality: personal freedom and interpersonal beneficence.

I. MORAL PROBLEMS OF PRIVATE PHILANTHROPY

Many questions about moral, and especially human, rights arise from private philanthropy as thus briefly characterized. These questions may be divided into three sets, which focus respectively on the *agents* of philanthropy (i.e., the philanthropists themselves), on the *recipients* of philanthropy, and on the *objects* for which philanthropic awards are given. First, regarding the agents: Do they have a right to all the wealth they possess? Have they accumulated this wealth in a way that has respected the moral rights of other persons? If the answer is negative, even in part, then in what morally valid sense is all the wealth in question theirs to give away, even if they use it for philanthropic purposes: Do they have a *right* to give it away as they choose?

It should be noted that this question about rights is independent of questions about the philanthropists' motivations. We are all familiar with psychological theories that seek to explain philanthropic activities by refer-ence to pangs of guilty conscience or demands of the superego, thirst for power or domination or at least for paternalistic control over the persons benefited, concern for reputation and furthering of business interests and profits, and so forth. It would be a mistake, however, so to generalize these explanations as to underestimate the ways in which private philanthropy may also be an expression of the milk of human kindness, the love of one's fellow human beings, and concern for furthering projects that are among the highest manifestations of distinctively human values and dignity. Nevertheless, entirely apart from these motivational considerations, there remains the prior and more basic question of whether the philanthropists have a right in the first place to the wealth they dispense for their beneficent objectives.

A second set of questions bears on the recipients of the philanthropists' gifts. We may begin with an issue that emerges from the first set of questions, but focuses not on the philanthropists' rightful ownership of their wealth but on the relation between their use of it and the rights of their recipients. Do the agents or philanthropists have a right to use the wealth they possess as they see fit without regard to the rights that other persons – their actual or potential recipients – might have to that very same wealth?

To see the point of this question, let us briefly consider the nature of the philanthropic relation. This relation is one of supererogation. In its simplest form, one person A freely gives to another person B some good X (usually but not always money), such that A has no strict moral duty to give X to B and B has, correlatively, no claim-right to receive X from A. Thus, A's gift to B is an act of generosity or charity. A would not be deserving of any severe censure, let alone coercion or punishment, if he or she refrained from giving X to B; and B, in turn, has no ground for demanding that A give him or her X, or for complaining if A fails to give him or her X. Thus, the relation among A, B, and X is one of complete freedom on the part of A both to act and to refrain from acting toward B in the way he does; and so far as B is concerned, obtaining X is entirely or almost entirely dependent upon A's free choice to give him X. The relation of A to B, then, is that of free, voluntary, purposive agent to passive, dependent recipient.

The question that arises here is whether the philanthropic relation as thus analyzed is always respectful of the rights of B, the recipient. May it not be the case that, at least with regard to certain X's, B has a right to receive them from A? If this were indeed the case, it would mean that the philanthropic relation must be supplanted by a relation between the respondent and the subject of *rights* or, correlatively, a relation whereby a person owes certain *strict duties* to other persons, so that the latter are in a position to justifiably demand or claim the X's in question from A, as against being in a position of passive dependence upon A's optional decision.

An important part of the point of this question can be brought out if we connect it with a third set of questions, which focus on the objects of philanthropy, i.e., the projects or purposes which the philanthropists seek to promote. Should these objects always be at the option of the giver or agent? Does his right to use his wealth as he sees fit always override other social values that might accrue from the wealth he possesses? This question becomes especially pressing when the other values include basic needs of persons. For example, *should* philanthropists – or even more starkly, do philanthropists *have a right to* – use their wealth to endow rare book libraries or art museums, let alone baseball picture collections or cat lovers' dispensaries, when millions of persons are starving? Indeed, can it not be soundly maintained that the starving persons have an *overriding right* to the resources in question?

It should be noted that while all three of these sets of questions deal with claim-rights, i e , rights which entail correlative duties on the part of respondents, the first set of questions deals with active and negative rights, while the second and third sets of questions deal with passive and positive rights. The rights in the first set of questions are active in that they are rights on the part of the philanthropists to do something, i.e., to give away their money as they see fit; and the rights are negative in that the correlative duties are that other persons simply refrain from interfering with the philanthropists' actions. The rights in the second and third sets of questions, on the other hand, are primarily passive in that they are rights to receive something, i.e., to receive money or goods from the philanthropists as a matter of entitlement, of what is the recipients' due; and the rights are positive in that the correlative duties involve positive actions on the part of the philanthropists. But despite these differences, all the rights in question are stringent claim-rights in that they entail strict duties whose nonfulfillment calls at least for severe censure and perhaps even for coercive sanctions.

The three sets of questions that I have briefly outlined raise, of course, many important and difficult moral issues. In order to cope with them, however, we must note that each of them rests on the assumption that the most fundamental consideration about the morality of philanthropy concerns matters of rights: the rights of the philanthropists, of their recipients, and of other persons. Underlying all three sets of questions, then, is this more basic question: Is their focus on rights sound? Should we really be asking about the rights of the philanthropists or of other persons, or should we be asking some other question instead, such as whether social utility or the social good is furthered or maximized by persons' philanthropic use of the resources they possess?

One of the grounds for asking this more basic question is that amid the enthusiastic endorsements that rights, especially human rights, have received in the modern world, there have been currents, going back at least to Burke, Bentham, and Marx, that have held that moral rights language is senseless, that it is a sinister cover for egoism, anarchy, or vested interests, and that the whole recent proliferation of claims to rights on behalf of various submerged groups in our society and our world is conceptually confused or morally illegitimate or both. Closely related to this charge is a further epistemological point. It is contended that, whereas the social consequences of philanthropic activities are readily ascertainable by empirical means, such ascertainment is not possible for rights: the determination of who has rights to what involves conflicts of basic moral principles whose resolution is difficult or impossible to achieve. From such considerations it may follow that it is a mistake to emphasize rights as heavily as I did in my original three sets of questions about the moral status of private philanthropy.

I now want to deal with these issues by presenting and arguing for three main theses. The first is that the concept of rights, and especially of human rights, is central and indeed indispensable to the whole field of morality, and that it can be shown by a rational line of argument that all persons have rights to certain kinds of objects, so that the focus on rights in my questions about philanthropy is sound. The second thesis is that these human rights are positive as well as negative; and as positive rights, they have as their objects certain economic goods which serve to limit the rights of philanthropists to dispose of all their wealth as they see fit. The third thesis, however, is that the positive rights in question are not themselves unlimited, so that they leave open a philanthropic "space" for the support of other values which may be determined by the philanthropists' free choices or preferences.

II. THE MORAL CENTRALITY OF RIGHTS

I turn, then, to my first main thesis: that the concept of rights, and especially of human rights, is central and indeed indispensable to the whole field of morality. Proof or argument is needed here, because some of the most familiar considerations that have been adduced for this thesis are quite inconclusive. For example, it has been held that social utility, the chief alternative to rights, cannot provide the basis of morality because it overlooks the "separateness of persons."[1] But this does not, of itself, establish the moral indispensability of rights, both because the "separateness" in question may fail to take account of the social and moral interdependence of persons and because it does not indicate what, if any, are the moral limits on the rights which reflect the "separateness" or inviolability of persons. Moreover, morality could be based on considerations that take account of the separateness of persons without adducing rights. For example, the focus could be on individual *preferences* or on the distinct *virtues* of individuals. It has also been

---

[1] See John Rawls, *A Theory of Justice* (Cambridge: Harvard University Press, 1971), pp. 27, 187; and Robert Nozick, *Anarchy, State, and Utopia* (New York: Basic Books, 1974), p. 33.

held that rights are "trumps"[2] in that they override all other kinds of moral considerations. But this, so far, is bare assertion, for which its exponents have given little or no argument. As such, it does not *prove* that rights are central, let alone indispensable or conclusive, for morality. Moreover, in the absence of principled argument, the "trumps" idea of rights can be upheld by thinkers as different as Dworkin and Nozick, the former affirming and the latter denying that persons have extensive positive rights to welfare. Hence, no determinate conception of the *contents* of rights is established by this idea.

Rights and Action

I shall now present an argument to show that the concept of rights, and especially of human rights, is central and indeed indispensable to morality. The argument will proceed through the connection of both morality and rights with *human action*. Specifically, I will show that morality logically involves the concept of action, and that action, in turn, logically involves the concept of rights.

The connection of morality with action is well known. For all moral and other practical precepts, despite their enormous variety, are concerned directly or indirectly to tell persons how they ought to act, especially toward one another. Hence, the general context of all morality is action.

The connection of action with rights is, in certain important respects, less well known. It is indeed clear that actions are among the main objects of rights, for moral as well as legal rights include rights to act in certain specific ways, for example, to move about freely, to express opinions, to join in association with other persons, and so forth. But what is less well known is that the concept of rights is crucial to all action, because the most fundamental rights of persons or, as they are also called, human rights, have as their objects the necessary conditions of action and successful action in general. What makes human rights so important is that without them, persons either cannot act at all or cannot act with general chances of success in achieving their purposes. From this it follows that if these rights are withheld or denied, then either persons are directly deprived of the conditions they need to have in order to be agents and successful agents in general, or else their possession of these conditions is rendered precarious and unstable.

Let me put this point in a related way. Human rights are justified requirements that all persons have certain important goods as their due, as what they are entitled to, as what they can justifiably demand that other persons respect either by noninterference or, in certain circumstances, by

---

[2] See Ronald Dworkin, *Taking Rights Seriously* (Cambridge: Harvard University Press, 1977), p. xi; and Nozick, *Anarchy, State, and Utopia*, p. ix.

positive assistance. And the contents of these goods are the necessary conditions of action and successful action in general. Thus, what human rights require is that these necessary goods not be removed or interfered with by any other persons or groups and, also, in certain circumstances, that these necessary goods be provided for all persons who cannot obtain them by their own efforts. Hence, human rights are normative property in goods that every person must have either in order to be an agent at all or in order to have general chances of success in fulfilling the purposes for which he or she acts. It is for this reason that human rights are uniquely and centrally important among moral concepts. For no morality, together with the goods, virtues, duties, and rules emphasized in diverse moralities, is possible without the necessary goods of action and successful action which are the objects of human rights.

There may, indeed, be other moral approaches to the necessary conditions of action and successful action that do not directly proceed in terms of rights. Utilitarianism is the most famous example of such an alternative approach. But in utilitarianism the central focus is not on the distributive question of what is due or owed to each person for his own sake, including especially each person's needs of agency. Instead, the basic moral criterion of utilitarianism is aggregative: actions and policies are morally right insofar, and only insofar, as they serve to maximize utility overall. Hence, in utilitarianism, individual rights, if they are accepted at all, are ancillary to and dependent on the attainment of the greatest whole of collective goods. But since such attainment may require the overriding of the individual's fulfillment of his own agency-needs, the rights of individuals are rendered precarious by the utilitarian criterion. Moreover, because what is at issue here is fulfillment of *necessary needs*, an approach in terms of individual *preferences* is insufficient: the relevant modality must be one of necessity, not of optionality or possibility. And the need-fulfillment must be what each actual or prospective agent normatively owns or has property in. Hence, the approach to morality in terms of the concept of human rights is indispensable if fulfillment of each person's needs of action, which are the central concern of morality, is to be the chief focus and primary criterion of moral rightness.

What I have said so far is perhaps already sufficient to establish my first main thesis, that the concept of rights, and especially of human rights, is central and indeed indispensable to the whole field of morality. But questions may still be raised on two interrelated points: first, whether the human rights do indeed have as their objects the necessary conditions of action and successful action in general; and second, whether such rights exist, i.e., whether all humans do indeed have rights to these necessary conditions.

I have elsewhere dealt with these two questions in considerable detail.[3] Here I want briefly to present what I think is the only kind of argument that can answer the questions successfully. This argument is *dialectical*, in that it involves showing that every agent logically must hold or accept that he or she and all other actual or prospective agents have rights to the necessary conditions of action and successful action in general. The argument for human rights, then, must in this way be agent-relative, i.e., relative to what every agent logically must hold or accept. This relativity to agents and their claims does not, however, remove the stringency either of the rights themselves or of the argument for their existence. For since agency is the proximate general context of all morality and indeed of all practice, and since all humans are actual, prospective, or potential agents, whatever is necessarily justified within the context of agency is also necessary for morality, and what logically must be accepted by every agent is necessarily justified within the context of agency. Because of this actional context, the moral conclusion that all humans equally have rights to the necessary conditions of action can then be stated assertorically as well as dialectically.

The Dialectical Argument for Human Rights

I shall now give a brief outline of how this dialectical argument for rights on the part of every agent proceeds. To begin with, we must be aware of what are the necessary conditions of action and successful action in general. For this purpose, it must be kept in mind that the sense of "action" which is relevant here is that which is the general object of all moral and other practical precepts. Taken in this sense, actions have two generic features and necessary conditions: *freedom* and *well-being*. Freedom is the procedural generic feature of action; it consists in controlling one's behavior by one's unforced choice while having knowledge of relevant circumstances. Well-being as here understood is the substantive generic feature of action; it consists in having the purpose-related general abilities and conditions that are required either for being able to act at all or for having general chances of success in achieving the purposes for which one acts. The components of such well-being thus fall into a hierarchy of goods, ranging from life and physical integrity to self-esteem and education.

I turn now to the proof of the dialectical proposition stated above: every agent logically must hold or accept that he or she and all other actual or prospective agents have rights to freedom and well-being. The argument is

---

[3] See Alan Gewirth, *Reason and Morality* (Chicago: University of Chicago Press, 1978); *Human Rights: Essays on Justification and Applications* (Chicago: University of Chicago Press, 1982); "The Epistemology of Human Rights," *Social Philosophy & Policy*, vol. 1, no. 2 (Spring 1984), pp. 1–24.

in two main parts. In the first part, I argue that every agent logically must hold or accept that *he or she* has rights to the necessary conditions of action and successful action in general. In the second part, I argue that each agent logically must admit that *all other agents* also have the same rights he claims for himself. Thus, the existence of certain universal moral rights, and thus of human rights, must be accepted within the whole context of action or practice.

The first part of the argument proceeds as follows. Since freedom and well-being are the necessary conditions of action and successful action in general, every agent must regard these conditions as necessary goods for himself, since without them he would not be able to act for any of his - purposes, either at all or with general chances of success. Hence, every agent has to accept (1) "I must have freedom and well-being." This 'must' is practical-prescriptive in that it signifies the agent's advocacy of his having the necessary goods of action, which he needs in order to act and to act successfully in general. Now, by virtue of accepting (1), every agent has to accept (2) "I have rights to freedom and well-being." For if he rejects (2), then, because of the correlativity of claim-rights and strict 'oughts,' he also has to reject (3) "All other persons ought at least to refrain from removing or interfering with my freedom and well-being." By rejecting (3), he has to accept (4) "Other persons may (i.e., it is permissible that other persons) remove or interfere with my freedom and well-being." And by accepting (4), he also has to accept (5) "I may not (i.e., it is permissible that I not) have freedom and well-being." But (5) contradicts (1). Since every agent must accept (1), he must reject (5). And since (5) follows from the denial of (2), every agent must reject that denial and accept (2) "I have rights to freedom and well-being." I shall call these *generic rights* because they are rights to have the generic features of action and successful action characterize one's behavior.

The first main part of the argument has thus established that all action is necessarily connected with the concept of rights. For every agent logically must hold or accept that he has rights to the necessary conditions of action and successful action in general.

Many questions may, of course, be raised about this argument. I have dealt with these questions elsewhere,[4] and the interested reader is invited to consult these other sources for additional analysis of the issues.

I turn now to the second part of the argument. On the basis of his having

---

[4] See Gewirth, *Reason and Morality*, pp. 82–102; *Human Rights*, pp. 67–78; "Why Agents Must Claim Rights: A Reply," *Journal of Philosophy*, vol. 79 (1982), pp. 403–410; "Replies to My Critics," E. Regis, Jr., ed., *Gewirth's Ethical Rationalism* (Chicago: University of Chicago Press, 1984), pp. 202–215; "Why Rights Are Indispensable," *Mind*, vol. 95 (1986), pp. 329–344.

to accept that he has generic rights, every agent also logically must accept that all other actual or prospective agents have these rights equally with his own. This generalization is an application of the logical principle of universalizability: if some predicate P belongs to some subject S because S has a certain quality Q (where the 'because' is that of sufficient condition), then P logically must belong to all other subjects S_1 to S_n that also have the quality Q. Thus, if any agent holds that he has the generic rights because he is a prospective purposive agent, then he also logically must hold that every prospective purposive agent has the generic rights.

Now every agent logically has to accept (6) "I have rights to freedom and well-being because I am a prospective purposive agent." For suppose some agent A were to object that the necessary and sufficient justifying condition of his having the generic rights is his having some property R that is more restrictive than simply being a prospective purposive agent. Examples of R might include his being a wage-earner or an entrepreneur or a banker or a landlord or an American or white or male or being named "Wordsworth Donisthorpe," and so forth. From this it would follow that A would logically have to hold that it is only his having R that justifies his having the generic rights, so that if he were to lack R, then he would not have them.

But such an agent would contradict himself. For we saw above that, as an agent, he logically must hold that he has the generic rights, since otherwise he would be in the position of accepting that he normatively *need not* have what he normatively *must* have, namely, the freedom and well-being that are the necessary conditions of action and successful action in general. Hence, since no agent, including A, can consistently hold that he does not have the generic rights, he must give up the idea that any such restrictive property R can be the necessary as well as sufficient justifying condition of his having these rights. From this it follows that every agent logically must acknowledge that, simply by virtue of being a prospective purposive agent, he has the generic rights, so that he also logically must accept (7) "All prospective purposive agents have rights to freedom and well-being."

Since this universalized judgment sets a prescriptive requirement for the action of every agent toward all other prospective purposive agents, who are or may be the recipients of his action, every agent logically must also accept for himself a moral principle which may be formulated as follows: (8) *Act in accord with the generic rights of your recipients as well as of yourself.* I call this the *Principle of Generic Consistency* (*PGC*), because it combines the formal consideration of logical consistency with the material consideration of the generic features and rights of action. This concludes the second part of the argument.

The argument for the *PGC* has thus dialectically established that human rights do indeed have as their objects the necessary conditions of action and successful action in general and that all humans, who are actual, prospective, or potential agents, do indeed have these rights. This, then, completes my argument for the first main thesis of this paper: the concept of rights, and especially of human rights, is central and indeed indispensable to the whole field of morality.

III.   POSITIVE RIGHTS TO BASIC WELL-BEING

The human rights as I have presented them so far are primarily negative, in that their correlative duties require that persons refrain from removing or interfering with the freedom and well-being of prospective purposive agents. I now turn to my second main thesis: the human rights are also positive, in that their correlative duties require giving help or assistance to persons who cannot attain basic well-being by their own efforts. Such well-being includes certain economic goods, and the positive rights to these serve to limit the rights of philanthropists to dispose of all their wealth as they choose.

The distinction between "negative" and "positive" rights has been criticized on the ground that the negative rights also require positive assistance from government. For example, the right not to be murdered or mugged calls for an active police force that provides protection for persons who need it.[5] This criticism makes an important point, but it does not remove the distinction between negative and positive rights. For the criticism overlooks the fact that the ground or justification for the positive assistance in question is to see to it that potential offenders *refrain from* the prohibited actions. Thus, the correlative duty that provides the ground for the positive assistance is itself still negative. The police, in this example, exist for the sake of assuring or facilitating fulfillment of the negative duty. Hence, the primary duty here is simply the negative one of refraining from murder or mugging, so that the correlative right is negative.

The positive rights to economic goods, as I shall now discuss them, do not have such negative duties as their primary ground. What they primarily require is not that persons refrain from certain kinds of actions but, rather, that persons perform certain kinds of actions that provide economic and related assistance for persons who cannot obtain certain basic goods by their own efforts. It may indeed be the case that the causes of the need for this assistance include the fact that governments and other institutions or groups have performed certain kinds of positive, subsistence-threatening actions, so that the economic rights in question require that the institutions refrain from such actions. Nevertheless, even in such cases the duty of directly alleviating

---

[5] See Henry Shue, *Basic Rights* (Princeton, NJ: Princeton University Press, 1980), pp. 37ff., 51.

the resulting needs involves giving positive assistance, not simply refraining from action as in the case of negative rights. Moreover, it is by no means clear that all cases of economic deprivation have such positive actions as part of their direct causal background.

To see how the human rights include positive rights to basic well-being, we must examine certain implications of the *PGC* for economic rights. According to the *PGC*, every prospective purposive agent, and thus every person, has equal rights to freedom and well-being as the necessary conditions of his or her action and successful action in general. The principle thus has two main requirements: one bearing on the right to freedom, the other on the right to well-being. Each of these requirements serves both to complement and to limit the other.

The Freedom Criterion

I shall not here discuss the right to freedom in any detail. As we have seen, freedom as a necessary condition of action consists in control of one's behavior by one's unforced choice with knowledge of relevant circumstances. Such freedom may be applied by the agent in many different kinds of actions. These actions or series of actions, whether engaged in by oneself alone or, as is far more usual, in combination with other persons, include the production of economic goods or commodities and voluntary exchange with other persons. Such uses of one's freedom result in a certain just distribution of economic goods: the goods are justly possessed by the persons who produce them or who acquire them by voluntary transfers or exchanges, so that they have property rights in those goods. This criterion includes, as an essential part, the traditional criterion of contribution: each person has a right to what he contributes to the productive process or to what voluntarily results from that contribution.

The freedom criterion as thus briefly sketched raises many difficult questions of interpretation and justification. In its application to the property rights of philanthropists and other wealthy persons, the questions include the following: How clearly can we identify the persons who produce various specific goods amid the enormous complexities of the actual productive processes in modern industrial societies? Do persons' abilities to perform their free productive actions, and the materials on which they work, derive only from the persons themselves or from a complex prior matrix of inheritance and social nurture, including education? In accumulating immense wealth, do persons violate the rights of other persons to economic goods? Also, there is a question about the freedom of persons at the opposite end of the scale: To what extent can persons' participation in the productive process be regarded as "free" when large numbers of them are driven by economic necessity to take jobs that are menial, degrading, exhausting, and health-threatening, and when they lack control over both the duration and the internal conditions of their work situation?

Such questions cast some doubt on the freedom criterion of economic rights insofar as that criterion purports to justify a person's right to *exclusive* possession of the commodities that "result from" his or her "voluntary" actions of production and exchange. And to this extent, the questions also cast some doubt on the right of philanthropists to dispose of their wealth as they desire.

The Need Criterion

I wish to focus now, however, on a different question about the economic sphere. It concerns the persons who do not participate at all in the productive process or in its fruits, or who do participate but only to an extent that does not enable them to fulfill their basic needs. All such persons lack, or are threatened with the lack of, the most basic part of what I have above called *well-being*. This brings us to the other main requirement of the *PGC*.

According to the *PGC*, all persons have equal rights to freedom and well-being as the necessary conditions of their action and successful action in general. We must now note that well-being itself falls into a hierarchy of three kinds of goods that are progressively less necessary for action. *Basic goods* are the essential prerequisites of action; they include life, physical integrity, health, mental equilibrium, and such specific goods as food, clothing, shelter, and medical care. *Nonsubtractive goods* are the general abilities and conditions needed for maintaining undiminished one's level of purpose-fulfillment and one's capabilities for particular actions. *Additive goods* are the general abilities and conditions needed for increasing one's level of purpose-fulfillment and one's capabilities for successful actions. Examples of nonsubtractive goods are not being lied to, stolen from, insulted, or threatened with violence. Examples of additive goods are self-esteem, wealth, and education. Persons' generic rights to these three kinds of goods are, respectively, *basic rights*, *nonsubtractive rights*, and *additive rights*. Of course, not all of these rights have governments as their respondents.

Now, for persons to participate in the productive process or in its fruits sufficiently to assure themselves a continued supply of basic goods, they must already have the basic goods, and they must also have relevant nonsubtractive and additive goods, including education. But many persons may be unable to participate in this way. They include some of the very young, some of the very old, the physically or mentally handicapped, the very ill, and the poorly educated. Other persons may suffer productive disabilities that, while less deep, may also threaten their supply of basic goods, because they are unemployed through no fault of their own, or because the commodities they produce are bought at prices which are not sufficient for their basic needs, or because drought or other natural conditions over which they have no control threaten them with starvation, or because they are or have been discriminated against on various unjustified grounds. In some of these cases, but not in all, the causal background of the inabilities in question includes positive actions by other persons or groups.

All persons who suffer from such productive disabilities, like all other prospective agents, have *positive rights* to well-being, and especially to basic well-being. This entails that other persons or groups, including the state, have correlative positive duties to provide relevant components of basic well-being for such persons insofar as the latter cannot provide them for themselves. The argument for there being such positive rights is parallel to the argument I outlined above for a negative right to both freedom and well-being. I shall now present a summary of the positive-rights argument.

Since basic well-being, in the sense indicated above, is a necessary condition of action and successful action in general, every actual or prospective agent has a general need for its components. Hence, every agent has to accept (1a) "I must have basic well-being." This "must" is practical-prescriptive in that it signifies the agent's advocacy of his having what he needs in order to act either at all or with general chances of success. Now, by virtue of accepting (1a), the agent also has to accept (2a) "I have a positive right to basic well-being." For if he rejects (2a), then, because of the correlativity of positive rights and strict positive 'oughts,' he also has to reject (3a) "Other persons ought to help me to have basic well-being when I cannot have it by my own efforts." By rejecting (3a), he has to accept (4a) "Other persons may (i.e., it is permissible that other persons) refrain from helping me to have basic well-being when I cannot have it by my own efforts." And by accepting (4a), he also has to accept (5a) "I may not (i.e., it is permissible that I not) have basic well-being." But (5a) contradicts (1a). Since every agent must accept (1a), he must reject (5a). And since (5a) follows from the denial of (2a), every agent must reject that denial and accept (2a) "I have a positive right to basic well-being."

The further steps of this argument are also parallel to the argument for negative rights. Each agent logically must admit that the sufficient reason or ground on which he claims positive rights for himself is that he is a prospective purposive agent, so he must accept the generalization that all prospective purposive agents have positive rights to basic well-being. Hence, he must also accept that he has positive duties to help other persons attain basic well-being when they cannot do so by their own efforts and when he can give such help without comparable cost to himself. When such help is needed by large numbers of persons, and especially when their needs have institutional roots, such help requires a context of institutional rules, including the supportive state.

In this way, I have argued that the duty to act in accord with the positive rights of other persons to fulfillment of their basic needs is rationally justified, so that it is morally right and indeed mandatory to provide help to basic well-being for other persons when they need this help and it can be given without comparable cost to the agent. I shall call this the *need criterion* of economic rights.

It will be noted that in the preceding argument, unlike the argument given earlier for negative rights to freedom and well-being, there is included an important addition, namely, the qualification (in steps (3a) and (4a)) that the agent cannot attain some aspect of basic well-being *by his own efforts*. This means that in the 'ought'-judgment (3a) he cannot rationally demand of other persons that they help him to have basic well-being unless his own efforts to have it are unavailing. For without this qualification there would not follow (5a) "I may not (i.e., it is permissible that I not) have basic well-being."

This qualification raises some complex problems about what efforts are actually available to persons and what their efforts can realistically accomplish. In view of the preceding argument for the *PGC*, there are negative moral limitations on the efforts that persons may justifiably exert in order to attain their own basic well-being; for example, they may not kill other innocent persons for this purpose, although, if conditions become sufficiently desperate, they may steal from them. But from the other side, there are questions about what degrees of effort may be justifiably demanded of persons within the context of available resources. For example, may persons be asked, within an economy of abundance, to work for very low, close-to-starvation wages in order to avert their actual starvation?

In considering such questions, it is important to keep in mind that basic well-being includes more than mere life; it also involves such necessary goods as the maintenance of health, which requires adequate levels of food, clothing, and other necessities, including a physically healthful environment. Within the limits of available resources, there must also be an assurance of continued supplies of such goods. Hence, persons have positive rights to the help of others if by their own efforts they are incapable of maintaining this assurance while other persons are able to provide it out of their surplus. There are also additive goods, such as education, which are directly helpful, not for basic well-being but for enabling persons to increase their levels of purpose-fulfillment. Since, however, education is a prime means of helping persons to maintain their basic well-being by their own efforts, including their acquisition of productive skills, the positive rights extend also to such means so far as they are available.

What this argument shows is that, on the basis of the necessity of well-being for action and successful action in general, no actual or prospective agent can rationally deny that he has a positive right to basic well-being and that he has a duty to provide for others when they need such help and he is in a position to give it without comparable cost. As a rational being, he has especially to recognize that there may be times when his own life, subsistence, and other aspects of his basic well-being may be threatened, so that he may then need the help of others because he cannot have or maintain his basic well-being by his own efforts. This point applies even against the kind of rugged individualist whom Sidgwick described as "a man in whom the spirit of independence and the distaste for incurring obligations would be so strong that he would choose to endure any privations rather than receive aid from others."[6] Sidgwick himself presented the qualification that "every one, in the actual moment of distress, must necessarily wish for the assistance of others." In any case, the point at issue here depends not on contingent psychological attitudes but, rather, on what is logically involved in rational purposive agency, where such agency is defined in terms of the common contents of all moral and other practical precepts.[7] Such agency aims at the fulfillment of a wide range of purposes and hence aims, at least dispositionally, at having the general necessary conditions of such fulfillment. It is for this reason that the implicit claim to positive rights to basic well-being is logically attributable to every actual or prospective agent. And these rights entail correlative positive duties to fulfill such rights.

IV. SCOPE AND LIMITS OF PRIVATE PHILANTHROPY

The preceding analysis has indicated that there are significant limits on the rights of philanthropists to dispose of their wealth according to their own preferences. Other persons have positive rights to some of that wealth if, by their own efforts, they cannot maintain and assure their basic well-being and other relevant components of well-being. Because of these positive rights, there are correlative strict duties to provide persons in need with basic goods. From this it follows that the philanthropic relation, insofar as it is supererogatory, must yield precedence to a mandatory relation in which persons are required, through taxes, to share their wealth to the degree necessary to fulfill the basic needs of other persons who cannot fulfill them by their own efforts.

The Primary Responsibility of the State

It is conceivable that the needs in question could be provided for by philanthropists acting freely out of compassion and charity. Such action would indeed be highly desirable and commendable. Nevertheless, it is

---

[6] Henry Sidgwick, *The Methods of Ethics*, 7th ed. (London: Macmillan and Co., 1907), p. 389n.

[7] See Gewirth, *Reason and Morality*, pp. 25, 46–47, 78, 81, 96–97, 169–170; and *Human Rights*, pp. 24–26.

important to keep in mind that fulfillment of basic needs is something to which persons who are in the condition described above are entitled as a matter of rights. There are two main points here. First, because the objects in question are necessary goods, the applicable modality is one of necessity, not of contingency or optionality; hence, the appropriate moral category is one of strict duties or requirements, not of generosity, charity, or mere permissions. Second, because these objects are owed to persons as their due and for the persons' own sakes, the directly appropriate moral category is one of rights.

The strict duties correlative with these rights might be fulfilled in different ways. But there are at least three reasons why the state should be the primary respondent of persons' positive rights to basic well-being. First, the basic goods and opportunities in question must be securely provided as needed; hence, if they are left to the optional decisions of willing private persons or groups, sufficient funds may not be given. Second, the benefits of these arrangements must be equitably and impartially distributed to the persons who need them without discrimination based on the variable preferences of potential providers. Third, the duty to contribute to such arrangements through taxes must also be equitably distributed to all the persons who have the required economic resources, in proportion to their ability. To leave the fulfillment of this duty solely to voluntary groups would allow many persons to shirk their duty. Thus, the positive moral rights to basic well-being should also be positive legal rights enforced by the state. But their legality rests on the moral rightness of subjecting property rights to the more imperative rights that are concerned with basic well-being.

The state's relation to these positive rights should not, however, be one of mere coercion, whereby the required taxes are exacted by law. It should also involve civic education wherein more fortunate persons are made aware of their obligations on behalf of the needy and brought to recognize the justice of the laws that enforce these obligations.

From the fact that individuals' property rights may be overridden in certain circumstances, however, it does not follow that there are no property rights at all. The empirically-based assumption here is that, insofar as some persons cannot fulfill for themselves the essential needs subserved by basic rights, other persons can provide this out of their surplus while still preserving the bulk of their property. None of this, however, amounts to anything like complete expropriation; the provision is not open-ended, so property rights remain, and with them the right of philanthropists to use their surplus as they choose. My position is hence not the same as John Rawls's "difference principle," according to which economic inequalities are unjustified unless they work out to the maximum benefit of the least advantaged.[8] This

[8] See Rawls, *A Theory of Justice*, pp. 75ff.

principle would permit and, indeed, require constant interference with persons' property in order to benefit maximally the least advantaged, thereby violating the claims of contribution or desert based on voluntary effort and accomplishment. My doctrine, on the other hand, requires only strictly limited redistribution to satisfy basic needs and to enable disadvantaged persons to attain abilities with which they can support themselves.

Of the many objections that may be raised against this thesis, I shall here consider two opposed views that bear especially on the rights of private philanthropists. According to one objection, there is no justification for limiting the rights of philanthropists over their wealth by reference to the basic needs of other persons. According to the other objection, even the basic needs of other persons are so boundless that philanthropists have no right to use any of their excess wealth at all for purposes other than the relief of such needs.

Conflicts Between the Rights to Freedom and to Well-being

To grasp the first objection, we must note that the positive right to basic well-being as briefly delineated above is in at least potential conflict with the right to freedom. For while the right to freedom involves, as we have seen, a right to exclusive possession of the economic goods one produces or receives by free transfer or exchange, the positive right to basic well-being requires that affluent persons, including would-be philanthropists, give up some of their goods, or the money equivalents thereof, to provide for the well-being of needy persons. As many libertarians have pointed out, this requirement, especially when it is enforced by law, is a restriction on the right to freedom, since it imposes on persons a legal as well as a moral duty they may not want to accept. But why is it justified to infringe the right to freedom of some persons in order to fulfill the right to basic well-being of other persons? Isn't this to use the former persons as mere means for the latter?[9]

To see how these questions are to be answered, we must recur to the justificatory basis of the generic rights. As we have seen, these rights have as their objects the necessary conditions of action and of successful action in general. From this derives one of the main bases of the resolution of conflicts of rights, which I shall call the *criterion of degrees of needfulness for action*. When two rights are in conflict with one another, that right must take precedence whose object is more needed for action. This is why, for example, the right not to be lied to is overridden by the right not to be murdered if the latter right can be fulfilled only by infringing the former. As I noted above in connection with the right to well-being, its components of basic, nonsubtractive, and additive rights fall into a hierarchy of progressively less needed conditions of action.

[9] See Nozick, *Anarchy, State, and Utopia*, pp. 30–33, 170, 179n., 238.

Now the kinds of freedom also fall into such a hierarchy. 'Freedom' should not be used as a global, undifferentiated concept. There is a distinction between occurrent or particular freedom and dispositional or long-range freedom, and also between different objects of freedom. A temporary interference with a relatively minor freedom, such as a traffic light, is morally less important than a long-range interference with the freedom to perform some highly valued action. Hence, if the affluent, including would-be philanthropists, are taxed so that a relatively small part of their wealth is removed in order to prevent the destitute from starving, this is a far less significant interference with their freedom than would be the case if they were forced to surrender most of their wealth or were prohibited from supporting political parties, religions, or universities of their choice. Objections that might be raised against this position because of the alleged impossibility of interpersonal comparisons of utilities are readily answerable by the consideration of levels of goods that enter into the argument for the *PGC*. Thus, it is not freedom in general that welfare rights restrict. By the same token, the right to freedom in the use of one's surplus property is not absolute; it may be overridden by other rights such as the rights to life, health, or subsistence, since the objects of the latter rights are more pressing because they are more needed for action.

The specific point, then, is that possession of a surplus of economic goods is less needed for action than are basic well-being and such additive goods as education. This is why property rights in the surplus are overridden by the basic and other rights in cases of conflict.

Persons are not treated as mere means, nor is their rationally justifiable freedom violated, when they are taxed in order to help other persons who are suffering from economic privation. For the principle underlying the taxation of the affluent to help others is concerned with protecting equally the rights of all persons, including the affluent. The *PGC*'s requirement that agents act in accord with the generic rights of their recipients entails that all prospective purposive agents must refrain from harming one another (according to the principle's criteria of harm) and also that in certain circumstances they must help one another if they can. Hence, limitations on their freedom to abstain from such help are rationally justified. The facts that only some persons may actually be threatened with harm or need help at a particular time, and that only some other persons may be in a position to inflict harm or to give help, do not alter the universality of the *PGC*'s provision for the protection of rights. Such protection is not only occurrent, but also dispositional and a matter of principle; it manifests an impartial concern for any and all persons whose rights may need protection. Hence, the *PGC*'s requirement for taxing the affluent involves treating all persons as ends, not merely as means. It also involves, as an essential part of this relation, that those who are taxed recognize their rationally grounded obligations on behalf of the needy and support the legislation that effectuates these obligations.

The Apparent Open-Endedness of Positive Rights

A second objection against my thesis about positive rights to basic well-being concerns the limits of the duties imposed by such rights. In view of the millions of persons who are starving in various parts of the world or who are otherwise threatened in their basic well-being by disease, torture, homelessness, and other harms or evils, doesn't the thesis that persons have positive rights to basic well-being entail that other persons who are more affluent or fortunate, including all would-be philanthropists, have correlative strict duties to engage ceaselessly in acts of succor or rescue? Thus, it is objected that philanthropic activities, far from being supererogatory even in part, must instead be entirely mandatory, both as to their occurrence and as to their contents. Especially in light of the vast numbers of afflicted persons, the positive right to basic well-being leaves no room for optional philanthropy or for any other optional ordinary activities. Instead, it imposes an "overload": unlimited, open-ended positive obligations that require a drastic, indeed, a revolutionary change in our whole way of life.[10]

This contention derives part of its moral cogency from our revulsion against the sharp, agonizing divisions between the haves and have-nots within each country and in the world at large. But there are serious shortcomings in the moral precept of unlimited positive duties that issues from the contention. The precept overlooks the causal context of the problems it addresses; hence, it also overlooks the appropriate mode of response.

It is vitally important to distinguish between isolated, individual acts of rescue, like throwing a rope to a drowning person, and large-scale evils like famine, to which the above contention primarily refers. The latter are not merely individual phenomena to be coped with, let alone solved, by individual actions. On the contrary, the phenomena in question have largely institutional, and specifically political, causes, and hence are to be dealt with by political and other institutional means. These means, moreover, do not require anything as dramatic or extensive as the complete curtailment of other personal projects, or the expropriation of all existing property beyond a bare minimum that would reduce all persons to a level close to that of the impoverished millions. The appropriate mode of response will vary from

---

[10] See James S. Fishkin, *The Limits of Obligation* (New Haven, CT: Yale University Press, 1982); and Peter Singer, "Famine, Affluence and Morality," *Philosophy & Public Affairs*, vol. 1, no. 3 (Spring 1972), pp. 229–243. The term "overload" is from Fishkin, ch. 18, pp. 145ff. See also Martin C. McGuire, "The Calculus of Moral Obligation," *Ethics*, vol. 95 (January 1985), pp. 199–223.

one specific problem to another. But the focus must be on the specific institutional causal factors and on the political and other changes that can serve to affect these factors.

It might be thought that the political means in question are merely vehicles for channeling the rescue efforts of individuals, so that the problems of "overload" still persist. After all, if the state acts as the representative of individual benefactors and rescuers, then the massive, boundless numbers of the needy who have positive rights to basic well-being would still require a boundless set of positive duties of rescue.

This reductive conception is faulty, however, for at least two reasons. One, which is closely connected with the arguments given above for the state's primary responsibility for fulfilling positive rights, bears on the factual effects of state action. Such action can yield enormous economies of scale, in that, because the resources that are put to use are so large by comparison with the resources available to each individual separately, a certain quantity of resources can accomplish far more when applied collectively by the state than when that same quantity is applied distributively by a number of individuals acting separately. For an obvious example of this difference, consider the way in which the state could commandeer a large number of airplanes or ships to transport food to starving millions, as against the efforts of one or many individuals acting separately to transport the same amount of food. Thus, when the problems of massive deprivation are tackled by state action, this can sharply reduce the contributions that are required from each individual, and the "overload" of obligations can be avoided.

A second shortcoming of the attempt to reduce state action to the action of individuals bears on the normative effects of operations of assistance or rescue, that is, on what those effects ought to be, what the operations ought to aim at accomplishing. When massive phenomena of deprivation occur, consisting in infringements of positive rights to basic well-being, the appropriate remedies must consist not simply in occurrent actions of rescue – although in the short term these may indeed be required – but also in correcting the institutional framework that generates or at least exacerbates the infringements in question. Thus, it is not enough to respond to each separate occurrence of famine without consideration of the underlying causes. Instead, these causes must themselves be attacked; and insofar as they are institutional or systemic, the remedies must also be institutional or systemic.

I shall briefly illustrate these considerations with a recent Oxfam report about the recurrent famines in the Sahel countries. As summarized in the *New York Times*, the report points out that the "standard response to famine" has been "for donor countries and local governments to rush in food for the dying." The report continues: "But it is seldom that there is an actual shortage of food in a country during a famine. The crisis is primarily one of marketing and maldistribution of food crops, not simply one of insufficient agricultural production." An important cause of this maldistribution (in the *Times*'s summary of the Oxfam report) is that "all the millions spent by local governments and the United Nations to expand commercial export crops such as peanuts, cotton and rice has [*sic*] decreased food production without boosting incomes enough for people to buy imported staples. These programs. . .have been driving smaller farmers off better lands and onto marginal fields. . . . These hardships are made worse by the low food prices set by the Sahel governments to aid urban residents. Such prices not only discourage farmers from producing food crops but also leave them without enough cash to fertilize fields or maintain equipment."

The solution to this problem, according to the Oxfam report as summarized in the *Times*, lies in "directing most technical aid to small farmers. And the best means of using this aid. . .is through the formation of village and regional cooperatives, in which these producers jointly protect their lands, share water supplies and, more important, gain a fair price for grains and animals by marketing them as a group."[11]

The policy proposals of the Oxfam report may underemphasize the specifically political difficulties of effecting the needed changes, including the indifference and even hostility of ruling elites to the basic needs of suppressed classes in the respective countries. But the appropriate remedies, in any case, including the ability of farmers to "jointly protect their lands," are a far cry from the near-impoverishment endorsed for individual rescuers by the "overload" conception of positive obligations. As a political project, the positive rights of the persons threatened by starvation require certain political changes, including more control by local farmers over their producing and marketing activities. These changes are a matter, first, for indigenous forces within each nation, and second, for the enlightened support of other nations and international organizations. The positive duties to work for such changes are a specific institutional response to the institutional causal factors adduced by the Oxfam report, including the vast amounts of money spent by local governments to expand commercial export crops and the low prices set by these same governments for the food produced by the farmers within each country.

---

[11] Seth S. King, "In Africa, A Natural Disaster Made Worse by Man," *New York Times*, June 17, 1984, Sec. E, p. 8. For similar analyses, see Thomas T. Poleman, "World Food: A Perspective," *Science*, vol. 188 (May 19, 1975), pp. 515ff; Pierre R. Crosson, "Institutional Obstacles to World Food Production," *Science*, vol. 188 (May 19, 1975), pp. 522, 523; Harry T. Walters, "Difficult Issues Underlying Food Problems," *Science*, vol. 188 (May 19, 1975), p. 530. See also Amartya Sen, *Poverty and Famines* (Oxford: Clarendon Press, 1982), and Shue, *Basic Rights*, pp. 41ff.

These considerations are reinforced by the *PGC*'s focus on the needs of agency. As I have indicated elsewhere,[12] transfers of food and other basic necessities to starving persons in other nations are indeed morally required in cases of emergencies. But, apart from emergencies, what is also needed is greater democratization within each country, so that governments will be more responsive to the needs of all their citizens and hence less prone to impose or accept enormous sacrifices from some for the sake of other, wealthier segments of the population. So far as concerns aid by foreign governments, this should proceed not by maintaining a relation of recipience and dependence on the part of the nations that are helped but, rather, by enabling them to develop and use their own resources – personal, political, and environmental. The point of such a policy, in keeping with the *PGC*'s concern for the conditions of agency, is not to reinforce or increase dependence but, rather, to give support that enables persons to maintain these conditions for themselves. On the national level, similarly, welfare assistance must be aimed not only at alleviating the immediate hardships and shortages of poverty and other handicaps but also at helping the poor and other disadvantaged persons to develop for themselves the ability to procure goods and services by their own efforts and thus to improve their capabilities for successful agency.

It is important, then, to reject a purview that assumes a permanent class of welfare dependents (whether domestic or international), with a permanent division between affluent agents or rescuers and poor, dependent recipients. Instead, the *PGC*'s emphasis on the rights of agency requires that all persons have the necessary conditions of action, including property, and that welfare programs (whether domestic or international) aim at fostering for all persons their acquisition of the conditions and abilities needed for successful agency and, hence, a cessation of exclusive dependence on others for basic goods. Such an aim requires not the kind of open-ended self-sacrifice envisaged in the "overload" conception of positive duties but, rather, a more finite set of institutional policies that are based on an analysis of the specific static and dynamic steps that can fulfill the positive rights in question.

These considerations indicate that there is a mean between the extremes of the "overload" conception of unlimited positive duties, on the one hand, and complete indifference or laissez faire, on the other. In assigning to political instrumentalities the effectuation of needed changes, I have no intention of discouraging individual concern, advocacy, and other involve-

---

[12] Alan Gewirth, "Starvation and Human Rights," *Human Rights*, pp. 197–217. On the broader issues, see also Gewirth, "Economic Justice: Concepts and Criteria," K. Kipnis and D. T. Meyers, eds., *Economic Justice: Private Rights and Public Responsibilities* (Totowa, NJ: Rowman and Allanheld, 1985), pp. 7–32; and "Economic Rights," *Philosophical Topics*, vol. 14 (Fall 1986), pp. 169–193.

ment. But such involvement must take realistic account of relevant causal, institutional factors, and it must not operate in such a way as to stifle or discourage the development of free productive agency on the part of the persons helped. In addition, individual rescuers must carry on their own productive employment both in order to generate the income from which can come the taxes to help pay for the institutional remedies and in order to maintain the whole context of free purposive action whose rights constitute the ultimate justification for the operations of government.

The appropriate scope for private philanthropy is determined by these considerations. For the agglomerations of vast wealth represented by the major foundations which constitute the most important segment of private philanthropy, the primary obligation, within the limits set by the state's responsibility for fulfilling basic needs, must be to encourage research and practical work aimed at understanding and remedying the threats to basic well-being that disfigure so much of the world. These threats are of two main kinds. One may be called *public evils* (on the analogy of "public goods"). These are afflictions against basic well-being that, if they affect some members of a community or society, affect all the members. Examples are nuclear war and environmental pollution. The other kind of threat may be called *discriminative evils*. These may afflict some members of the society without afflicting all. The famine on which I have focused above is an example of this; other examples are such economic and other deprivations as unemployment, homelessness, and disease. Private philanthropy can help to identify and to cope with many other areas of social need, and can thus supplement state action in many fruitful ways.

It is not too much of an idealization to say that the great private foundations in the United States have done much to fulfill their obligations regarding such serious threats to basic well-being. Hence, the tax-exempt status of these foundations is justified. Eminent examples are the Rockefeller Foundation's contribution to the development of the "green revolution" and the Ford Foundation's sponsorship of research into the problems of the inner cities.

In addition, private philanthropy can also promote other important human values, especially since, while the objects of human rights are the most basic and necessary conditions of human dignity, they do not exhaust all its contributory conditions. For example, the goods of intellectual and aesthetic culture are important parts of what I have called additive well-being, in that they help to increase persons' capabilities for successful action by, among other things, affording deeper insights into the values that make human life worth living. The support of these values must not, indeed, take precedence over the basic well-being which constitutes the essential prerequisites of human action. Nevertheless, private philanthropy has an important part to play in assisting the realization of all of these components of human well-being. This is especially the case since, as we have seen, the positive duties that are correlative with human rights are not infinite or open-ended; there is room for other moral activities as well.

Besides these considerations about the objects of philanthropy, there are formal reasons, from the side of modality, that also argue for there being a distinct moral place for private philanthropy. The very voluntariness and optionality of private philanthropy gives it an important moral status, parallel to the encomia that de Tocqueville proclaimed 150 years ago for the voluntary associations that he held to be distinctive of America as a democratic society. A constitutional democracy must indeed allow maximal freedom consistent with nonviolation of other rights, and private philanthropy is an important expression of such freedom. Moreover, a society without private philanthropy would be a morally impoverished society because it would lack the elements of spontaneous generosity and effectively benevolent fellow-feeling that are priceless aspects of human community. The Greek concept of *philanthropia* is closely related to the Biblical injunction to *love* thy neighbor, and the practical promotion of this love provides a valuable supplement to the mandatoriness of the rules and partly adversarial norms that uphold human rights.

Philosophy, University of Chicago

THE ROLE OF PRIVATE PHILANTHROPY IN A FREE AND DEMOCRATIC STATE

By Baruch Brody

This paper will attempt to defend the thesis that it is impossible to understand the proper role of private philanthropy in a free and democratic society without examining certain fundamental questions about the proper roles of the state and about the rights and obligations of owners of private property. It will defend that thesis by presenting arguments for four subordinate theses: (a) there are historical and philosophical reasons for being skeptical about the role of private philanthropy in a free and democratic state; (b) these reasons can be met by certain familiar responses, but these responses are not fully satisfactory; (c) certain radical libertarian views, and more moderate versions of those views, would provide a basis for an alternative understanding of the role of private philanthropy in a free and democratic state; (d) whether or not one accepts those views, one can also better understand that role if one adopts a view of the state which emphasizes its role in the promotion of the virtues.

(1) *Historical and Philosophical Doubts*

The skeptical challenge to the claim that there is an important role for private philanthropy in a free and democratic state can be put very simply. It is the challenge that the emergence of strong but democratic states, with the concurrent emergence of a proper understanding of the extensive nature of legitimate state functions, has undercut the need for private philanthropy and its corresponding favorable tax treatment. It is the further claim that these developments, both historical and conceptual, have left private philanthropy with no significant role. Let me elaborate upon both the historical and conceptual points.

It is obviously true that contemporary democratic states provide a far more extensive set of services than were provided by earlier states. Examples abound. In all contemporary democratic societies, education is primarily funded by tax dollars, and not by fees or by private philanthropic gifts. This is certainly true at the primary and secondary level (leaving aside for now parochial schools and a few private schools), and is increasingly true at the university level. This is a major shift from the past, and there is no doubt that this public funding has been central to the rise of education as a good provided to all rather than to a privileged few. To be sure, private philanthropy remains important for the strong private sector of higher education (and even public universities are increasingly seeking some private help). But is that anything more than a residue (even if a substantial residue) of the past, a leftover from the days in which higher education was funded by private philanthropists for the benefit of a few? Again, in all contemporary democratic societies, health care is heavily funded by tax dollars and less by fees or by private philanthropic gifts. This is certainly true of health care for the indigent, and increasingly true (especially if one considers the tax aspects of health insurance) of health care for all citizens. This is a major shift from the past, and there is no doubt that this public funding has been central to increased access to health care for all. Private philanthropy is today even less important in health care than in education, and it is even easier to say that its role today in the provision of health care is truly a residue of the past.

I have given only two examples, but many more examples of the same phenomenon can be identified. This, then, is the historical version of the claim we are examining. In medieval and early modern times, the state provided few services to its citizens. Private philanthropy was needed to insure that at least some would receive many of the services whose provision we now take for granted. All of that has changed, because private philanthropy is incapable of insuring that these services are provided to all, and democratic societies are unwilling to see them provided only to some. The services in question are now provided by the state through the use of tax funds. There is no real continued need for private philanthropy.

The same argument can be made at a conceptual level. What is required is that we make certain assumptions about the proper role of the state and about the proper way in which the state should fund its provision of services. The following assumptions are widely held, implicitly or explicitly, and will serve as the basis for our discussion:

(1) There are many important goods which will not be efficiently provided by the private market, either because the individuals who would receive them are incapable of paying for them or because the goods in question cannot be efficiently provided privately because they are public goods, because their provision involves externalities, and so forth. The provision of these goods would, however, increase the general welfare because the benefits of their provision outweigh the costs of providing them. States have as one of their main functions the promoting of the general welfare. Therefore, free and democratic states should and do provide these goods to their citizens.

(2) The provision of these goods requires substantial funds, funds that can only be raised by taxation. A free and democratic state attempts to raise its tax funds fairly. Fairness in taxation is best understood as taxing people in proportion to their ability to pay, and that is best understood as taxing people

by a progressive tax on income (or, alternatively, on wealth). If fairness is to be maintained, it is important that significant amounts of income (or wealth) not be exempt from taxation.

The first of these assumptions is a powerful assumption about the proper role of the state. It sees the state as charged with the responsibility of promoting general welfare. Such an assumption is most natural in a utilitarian moral framework, but it need not be confined to that framework. The crucial point is that many of the historical functions of private philanthropy were also connected with the improvement of the general welfare. Think of our earlier examples of education and health care. It certainly seems as though the provision of education to the uneducated and health care to the sick promote the general welfare. If, then, we adopt assumption (1) about the proper role of the state, we have a powerful reason for the state's providing education and health care and not relying upon private philanthropy to do its job. Why should the state rely upon private philanthropy to do the state's job for it? Even independently, then, of the historical failure of private philanthropy to provide the benefits in question to all appropriate recipients, there are conceptual reasons for saying that the state should provide these goods. Given that historical failure, the case for the state's providing the goods in question seems overwhelming. So what room is left for private philanthropy?

The second of these assumptions is an equally powerful assumption. It charges the state with the responsibility of maintaining a fair system of taxation by allowing few exemptions from taxation. Exemptions from taxation shift part of the burden of promoting the general welfare from those who can most easily bear this burden to others. Now an important fact about private philanthropy in many societies is that donors receive tax benefits from their donations. Income and/or wealth used for philanthropy is sheltered from taxation, and shifts the burden to others. Why should that income and/or wealth be so sheltered? If the state is doing its job, aren't tax exemptions for charitable purposes unfair and unnecessary?

This last point deserves special consideration. One of the most important ways in which some democratic societies, including the United States, continue to show allegiance to the significance of private philanthropy is by providing special tax benefits to philanthropists and to the foundations they sometimes create. There are many who simply accept this type of tax benefit as clearly appropriate. This last point questions the legitimacy of that tax benefit. If private philanthropy is a residue of the past, then why should others bear a greater tax burden in order to help encourage private philanthropy? Notice that some who challenge the tax benefits of philanthropic donations do so on the grounds that this benefit continues a governmental expenditure – the expenditure of the lost tax revenues – that may or may not be appropriate. Our last point raises an even more fundamental challenge, because it claims that the equity of our tax system is challenged by the tax benefits in question.

These, then, are the historical and philosophical challenges to the role of private philanthropy in free and democratic societies. The rest of this paper will look at possible responses to these challenges.

(2) A Standard Defense

The basic strategy adopted by many friends of private philanthropy is very simple. They begin by accepting assumptions (1) and (2) about the role of the state and about how it should finance its role. They then go on to argue that there are some roles that private philanthropy can better serve and that favorable tax treatment is the way in which the state encourages private philanthropy to carry out these roles. In this way, they reserve a place for state-encouraged private philanthropy even in an extensive democratic state.

What are these roles that are best served by private philanthropy? They might be viewed as ways of promoting the general welfare, but ways which are not appropriate for state action. Several examples obviously come to mind:

(a) The support of religious programs and institutions. There are very good reasons why the state should not be in the business of supporting these programs even if they provide goods to many and in that way promote the general welfare. These are all the reasons that are normally given for keeping a strong dividing line between church and state. But the provision of these religious services cannot be adequately provided in the private market, even if some of the recipients might be willing to pay for these services. So private philanthropy is required to insure the funding for the provision of these services. To encourage such philanthropy, the state provides tax benefits to the philanthropist.

(b) The support of the development of new ideas and new forms of artistic expression. There are very good reasons why the state should be very careful about the ways in which it supports the development of ideas and forms of artistic expression. After all, the power of selectively providing financial support (and all such support will be, in a world of limited resources, selective) is the power of promoting certain ideas and forms of expression, thereby discouraging others. So such programs of financial support by the state raise many concerns about freedom of thought and expression. But the support of the development of new ideas and new forms of artistic expression is central to promoting the general welfare. Now the private market may do a bad job in supporting these ideas and forms of expression, because the goods produced are in many ways public goods. So private philanthropy is required to insure the funding of these developments. To encourage such philanthropy, the state provides tax benefits to the philanthropists.

(c) The support of gaps in the provision of services by the state. For a variety of reasons, the state may fail to provide some of the services necessary for the public welfare but not properly provided by the private market. This may be due to an unwillingness to raise the tax funds required to provide those services, or it may be due to a failure to understand that these are services which the state needs to provide. Whether the gap is caused by a lack of understanding or a lack of funding, it needs to be filled if the general welfare is to be promoted. By the very nature of this case, this is a gap that will not be filled either by the state or by the private market, and can only be filled by private philanthropy. To encourage such philanthropy, the state provides tax benefits to the philanthropists.

A few examples might be of help at this point. Obviously, donations to churches, parochial schools, missions, and other religious activities fall under class (a). Philanthropic support of performing arts groups (opera, ballet, symphony, and theatre companies), of museums, and of research centers and think tanks are just three examples of philanthropies that fall under class (b). Finally, philanthropic support of educational institutions, of medical research groups, and of social service agencies (e.g., counseling agencies, agencies that provide services to the handicapped and homebound, agencies such as the Red Cross that provide emergency help) are examples of philanthropies that fall under class (c), since the state does provide some services of that type and could provide much more without raising any of the special problems of church-state relations and of state advocacy of ideas and/or forms of artistic expression.

There is an obvious objection lurking at this point about the tax-exemption encouragement of such philanthropic giving. It runs as follows: Suppose that the tax benefits of philanthropic giving average out to 30 percent of the gift. Suppose, in other words, that the donor is on the average giving 70 percent of the gift and the government is on the average giving 30 percent of the gift. Doesn't that involve, in cases of philanthropy of type (a) and type (b), objectionable state support of religious activities and objectionable state support of some – but not all – ideas and forms of artistic expression? So how can we have tax-benefit encouragement of philanthropies of types (a) and (b)? That problem does not arise in philanthropy of type (c), but other problems arise there. After all, if the state through its democratic processes has not decided that the gaps in question are real gaps which it wishes to fill, why should it be committed to providing some portion of the support for providing those services just because some private individual wishes to provide the rest? In short, this objection argues that we have not justified a favorable tax treatment of philanthropy even if we have found some important roles for private philanthropy.

I think that this objection, while initially very persuasive, can at the end be met. Let me at least suggest a way of doing so, a way that begins by distinguishing cases of types (a) and (b) from cases of type (c) and responds differently for these different cases.

What is the objection to state support of religious activities and of the development of new ideas and new forms of artistic expression? Many different answers can be given to this question, but suppose that the crucial answer to this question is that a free state should preserve a neutral posture in the areas of religion, ideas, and forms of artistic expression. Is that neutrality really compromised if the state supports any type of these activities in proportion to the willingness of individual citizens to support them? Would it not be better to see this form of support as the best way in which the state can, in the most neutral fashion, encourage these activities which are so important for the promotion of the general good? And if so, isn't this why tax-benefit encouragement of private philanthropy of types (a) and (b) is not objectionable, precisely because it represents an appropriately neutral way for the state to fulfill its role, rather than an unfair exemption of some income and/or wealth?

The objection in the case of philanthropy of type (c) can be met in a different way. One of the things that we must all recognize, even if we are firm believers in democratic decision making, is that democratic decision making often fails to produce optimal results, either because it fails to properly identify needs and ways of meeting them or because the players lack the courage to raise the taxes required to meet the needs. How shall we meet this problem? One way of doing so is to allow individuals to act to fill what they perceive to be gaps, and to encourage them by some state tax benefit. In short, tax-benefit encouragement of private philanthropy of type (c) is a way of meeting a problem with democratic decision making, rather than a way of helping private individuals overrule democratic decisions. Therefore, it is not objectionable precisely because it represents an appropriate way for the state to fulfill its role rather than an unfair exemption of some income and/or wealth.

We have seen, therefore, that it is possible to develop a powerful defense both of the role of private philanthropy and of government encouragement of it through favorable tax treatment. Notice that this defense is made even granting the very assumptions (1) and (2) which were the basis for the challenge I presented in section (1) of this paper.

I am, nevertheless, not satisfied with this defense. There are two bases for my dissatisfaction. The first is that this defense of private philanthropy rests on too many claims which are open to doubt. The second is that it makes private philanthropy too peripheral to a picture of the good society. Let me elaborate upon each of these points.

Consider, for example, the argument for private philanthropy of type (a), the support of religious programs and institutions. Spelled out carefully, that argument involved the following steps:

(i) the provision of religious services by religious institutions is essential to the promotion of the general welfare, and the state should therefore be concerned to see that these services are provided;

(ii) direct state funding of these institutions to provide these services is open to serious objection;

(iii) indirect state funding that encourages private philanthropy is not, so that is how the state should see to it that these services are provided.

Similar steps are involved in the arguments for private philanthropy of types (b) and (c), the support of the development of new ideas and new forms of artistic expression and the support of gaps in the provision of services by the state. My first problem is that each of these steps are open to significant doubt, so our defense of private philanthropy is too shaky.

What sort of doubts can be raised about each of the steps? Step (i) is particularly vulnerable in the defense of philanthropy of type (a), since it rests upon a claim about the beneficial impact of religious services. One might well question either the truth of that claim or the legitimacy of developing public policy in a free and democratic society upon the basis of such a claim. The analogous step in defense of philanthropy of types (b) and (c) is presumably less vulnerable. Step (ii) is vulnerable in the defense of philanthropy of both types (a) and (b). The existence in the United States of some direct state funding for the development of new ideas and new forms of artistic expression and the existence of democratic societies which provide direct state funding for religious services provided by religious institutions is sufficient to make us at least wonder whether or not the American commitment to (ii) represents anything more than blind dogma. Step (ii) is trivially true, however, for type (c) philanthropy. Step (iii) is extremely vulnerable in each case. Is indirect state funding really a way of maintaining neutrality among religions, ideas, and forms of artistic expression, or is it just a way of supporting those religions, ideas, and forms of expression which are supported by the more affluent portions of society? Is indirect state funding more likely to close gaps, as the defense assumes, or more likely to waste state funds in support of the whims of philanthropists? In short, our defense of private philanthropy faces too many challenges.

There is, moreover, another reason for being concerned about our defense, one that is more difficult to state but which seems to be extremely important. The defense of private philanthropy which I have offered still sees it as something residual, even if important. There are some projects which the state will not or should not handle directly, so private philanthropy with indirect state funding takes its place. The friends of private philanthropy should, I submit, want to find more central roles for it. In order to do so, however, they will need to proceed at a more fundamental level to criticize assumptions (1) and (2) about the role of the state and about the funding for a state.

(3) One Less Standard Defense

Central to the skeptical challenge to the role of private philanthropy were assumptions (1) and (2). So we must turn now to an examination of them. One way to challenge (1) would be to insist that it offers too broad a mandate for state action. If this mandate for state action were limited, perhaps there would be a broader role for private philanthropy.

A libertarian-oriented theory of the state would challenge the assumption that the state has as one of its main functions the promotion of the general welfare. It sees the state as having the more limited role of protecting the rights of individuals. No doubt this may also contribute to the general welfare, but libertarian-oriented theories would say (a) that individual rights need to be protected by the state whether or not their protection in a particular context promotes the general welfare and (b) that the state should not engage in other activities which promote the general welfare, particularly if that would mean violating any individual rights.

This approach to the role of the state certainly leads to a more limited conception of its role than the conception found in assumption (1). How much more limited? That depends, of course, upon your theory of rights. Strict libertarian thinkers believe that the rights we have are negative rights, rights not to be killed, not to be constrained in our liberty, and so forth. Other thinkers, whom we might call quasi-libertarian thinkers, extend their list of rights to include certain limited positive rights, rights to certain limited amounts of money or goods. In any case, much of what is currently provided by way of services by most democratic states would not be provided by libertarian or quasi-libertarian states.

How should such states fund the protection of rights, whether negative or positive? Libertarian and quasi-libertarian thinkers are badly split on that question, but one thing is clear. Such theorists find little attraction in the idea that taxation should be based upon the ability to pay, and are not therefore supporters of progressive taxes on income and/or wealth. This means that the exemption of some income and/or wealth from taxation, while leading to a breakdown of the correlation between tax burden and ability to pay, is not necessarily unfair or otherwise objectionable. So the adoption of such an approach would lead to a rejection of assumption (2).

Critics of libertarian theories of the state often argue that such theories are unconcerned with the potential decline in general welfare produced by the limited state's not providing many of the goods that the market will not provide, but whose provision contributes so much to the general welfare. Defenders of libertarian-oriented theories of the state often reply that the existence of the more powerful state is such a threat to freedom (and perhaps, therefore, to general welfare) that we are better off with the limited state. Both sides of this familiar debate miss the role of private philanthropy and the difference between the state provision of goods and the social provision of goods through nonmarket mechanisms. Since this is the central point for our purposes, let me elaborate upon it.

Purchasing goods in the market is one way in which individuals can receive these goods. Receiving the goods from the state, where the state funds that by tax dollars, is a second way in which individuals can receive these goods. But there is a third way, the way which is our concern in this paper, by which individuals can receive these goods. This is through the efforts of private philanthropy. Social encouragement of private philanthropy becomes a way in which society, but not the state, can provide goods through nonmarket mechanisms.

Why are libertarian-oriented thinkers opposed to the state provision of these goods? In part, because they do not see this as the function of the state. More important, however, is their view that tax funding for the provision of these goods, if these goods are not something to which the recipients have a right, results in taxpayers being illegitimately coerced to support the provision of these goods, and is a violation of their individual rights. Now none of this applies to the social provision of these goods through the encouragement of private philanthropy.

All of this leads us to a libertarian-oriented theory of private philanthropy which runs as follows: there are many goods which would not be efficiently provided by the private market, because the individuals who would benefit from their provision are incapable of paying for them, because the goods are public goods, because their provision involves externalities, and so forth. The efficient provision of these goods would, however, increase the general welfare. It would be inappropriate, nonetheless, for the state to provide those goods and fund that provision with tax dollars. Because the recipients have no right to these goods, forcing taxpayers to fund the provision of these goods would violate the rights of the taxpayers. The only morally legitimate way that will work for society to provide these goods is the encouragement of private philanthropy. So there is a major role for private philanthropy in a free democratic society, a role that becomes more and more significant as one becomes stricter and stricter in one's libertarian approach.

An example would be appropriate at this point. Consider public parks. Believers in assumption (1) would see the provision of public park space as one of the legitimate roles of the state, and would support state taxation to fund parks. The only role of private philanthropy in this area would be to supplement the state's provision of park space when philanthropists judged that the state had not provided enough. Libertarian-oriented thinkers would view this question very differently. The provision of park space through funds raised by coercive taxation would be illegitimate because the users of the park have no right to be provided with park space for their use. Unfortunately, relying merely upon the market provision of park space would exclude many who might most benefit from that space (the indigent who most need public park space). Private philanthropists who support the development of public parks provide this great benefit without infringing upon the rights of taxpayers. So society has every reason to encourage such private philanthropy.

Such examples can be multiplied over and over, because libertarian-oriented thinkers are not just talking about closing gaps which the state could legitimately have filled. For libertarian-oriented thinkers, then, private philanthropy is central to a properly structured society, for it is the vehicle for the social promotion of the general welfare, leaving just the protection of rights to the state.

To what extent should libertarian-oriented thinkers support the social encouragement of private philanthropy? In particular, should they support favorable tax treatment for philanthropic gifts? It is hard to answer that last question because there exists no generally accepted libertarian-oriented theory of taxation. But at least this much can be said: it will all depend upon whether the favorable tax treatment is viewed as an indirect government expenditure, ruled out on libertarian grounds, or as a legitimate exemption because the philanthropic use of the funds undercuts the libertarian-based reasons for taxing those funds.

I suspect that skeptics about private philanthropy will not be satisfied with this libertarian-oriented defense of it. Their dissatisfaction might be put as follows: however sound this defense may be conceptually, it fails to meet our original historically-based skepticism about private philanthropy. Did we not see that the philanthropic provision of goods important to the general welfare failed, and that state provision is required to insure that the general welfare is promoted? How, then, can anyone advocate on conceptual grounds a return to a system that failed in the past and which we have no reason to suppose will do better in the future?

Defenders of our libertarian-oriented approach should, I believe, offer two responses at this point. They are: (A) this historically-oriented skepticism is one-sided. It looks only at the contribution to the general welfare made by the state's assuming the role of providing these goods. A balanced assessment needs to take into account the other consequences of the rise of the state with a broader role, including the decline in general welfare due to the violation of the rights of taxpayers compelled to support these provisions of goods and the decline in general welfare due to the indirect effects of the welfare state to which libertarian-oriented thinkers often appeal. (B) This historically-oriented skepticism begs the question by assuming that the comparative success and failure of state and philanthropic provision of these goods is to be judged merely by the impact upon the general welfare. This utilitarian assumption should be rejected as based upon an unsound moral theory. A more proper comparative evaluation should focus upon the preservation of individual rights and freedoms, and that makes the entire comparison look very different.

In short, then, a second defense of the role of private philanthropy rejects the initial assumptions (1) and (2) of the skeptical challenge and uses libertarian-oriented alternatives as a basis for defending the role of private philanthropy. It avoids some of the questionable assumptions of the initial standard defense, and it makes private philanthropy very central to a free and democratic society. But it does rest upon strong libertarian-oriented views which many might reject. In the next section of this paper, we shall look at another defense which does not involve these libertarian-oriented views.

(4)   Another Less Standard Defense

We have so far examined two defenses of private philanthropy against the charges leveled by the skeptical challenge. One defense accepted the view of the state as the promoter of general welfare. A second was based upon a view of the state as the protector of individual rights. It should be no surprise that these are the conceptions of the state presupposed in our defenses. Contemporary moral and political theory has focused on the promotion of the general welfare and the protection of individual rights, and few other value themes have emerged that might serve as the basis for a different understanding of the role of the state and a different defense of private philanthropy. In this final section of the paper, we will look at another value theme, the virtues, to see whether a consideration of the virtues could be of help to us.

Ancient moral philosophy placed great emphasis on the moral virtues. Plato and Aristotle, for example, did not often discuss such questions as what rights people have or what actions will best promote the general welfare. They primarily discussed the question of what sort of people we ought to be and what sort of actions we ought to do as part of being people of that sort. Modern moral philosophy has paid much less attention to these questions. In the last few years, however, we have heard arguments to the effect that we ought to return to the morality of virtues as opposed to the morality of rights and of general welfare. I am not interested in such strong

claims; I am interested, however, in the suggestion that thinking about
virtuous people and virtuous actions, as a supplement to thinking about
individual rights and general welfare, could help us in developing an adequate moral and political theory and (what is relevant to the current context)
an adequate understanding of the role of private philanthropy.

There are many difficult questions about the virtues that we cannot begin
to deal with here but which should be noted. Among these are the following:
(1) Is it enough to have a certain virtue that one perform actions of a certain
sort, or must the actions in question be performed for the appropriate
motives? (2) Are all virtuous actions ones that we are already obliged to
perform (as a way of respecting the rights of others or promoting the general
welfare), or are there virtuous actions which have moral value just because
they are virtuous? (3) How does one weigh the virtuous character of an
action against other more traditional values of the action in trying to
determine which action one ought to perform?

Suppose now that someone held the following views: (A) virtuous people
and the virtuous actions which they perform are valuable in part because of
instrumental considerations and in part because of their intrinsic merit (the
answer to question (2) is very central in determining which is the greater
part); (B) one important role of the state is aiding the development of
virtuous people and the performance of virtuous actions; (C) for a variety of
reasons, laws compelling virtuous behavior are a bad way to aid in those
processes, but that does not prevent the state from developing alternative
ways of aiding the development of virtuous people and the performance of
virtuous actions. Such a person, I submit, would then have the philosophical
basis for still another defense of the role of private philanthropy in a free and
democratic society. Let me explain.

Philanthropic actions often display a number of different virtues. Gifts to
aid those in need, alleviating their suffering and deprivation, may be displays
of the virtue of compassion. Gifts to help promote causes, ideas, and forms
of expression to which one has a personal commitment may display the virtue
of personal integrity. Gifts which aid major public projects may display the
virtue of magnanimity. Gifts which defray the costs of providing a good from
which one benefits may display the virtue of fairness. Gifts to support
unpopular but deserving activities may display the virtue of courage. So
those who believe (A), who believe in the value of the virtues and of virtuous
actions, have every reason to value philanthropic actions. Particularly if one
believes that there are many virtuous philanthropic actions which have value
independently of their role in promoting general welfare and protecting
individual rights, one will have a new reason for valuing many philanthropic
actions.

(B) and (C) complete the defense of philanthropy. The state, by (B), has as one of its roles the promotion of these virtues and of the performance of these virtuous philanthropic actions. By (C), it cannot fulfill that mission by compelling the performance of virtuous philanthropic actions. What can it do instead to fulfill that mission? It can leave ample scope for private philanthropic activity by not preempting all occasions for its display, and it can encourage that activity by favorable tax treatment of such activities, the same way in which it encourages many other desirable activities. It should do so precisely because it recognizes the central importance of these private philanthropic activities.

There are many obvious ways to challenge this last defense of the role of private philanthropic activities. I want to focus on three, objections related to state promotion of morality, to the idea that the display of these virtues requires a broad scope for private philanthropy, and to tax benefits as a way of encouraging virtuous behavior. Let us look at each of these objections separately.

Much contemporary liberal and libertarian thought has been devoted to arguing for a strict distinction between morality and the law. In particular, extensive argumentation has been offered for the claim that the sanctions of the criminal law should not be used as a way to force people to perform certain actions and refrain from performing others simply because the actions in question are intrinsically right or intrinsically wrong. Isn't this conception of the state encouragement of virtuous actions because of their intrinsic desirability a way of bringing in through the back door of tax benefits what has been ruled out of the front door of laws requiring such behavior? Isn't my proposal just a new way of legislating morality? I think not. After all, the crucial objection to the use of the criminal law to enforce morality is that it is a way of coercing people to behave morally. No such coercion is involved here, since with the most generous of tax benefits ever proposed, we are at most simply relieving people of *some* (not *all*) of the burdens of behaving virtuously, and that can hardly be viewed as coercion.

Why do we need private philanthropy as a way of displaying these virtues? Can they not be displayed in other ways, most notably by people's political behavior? Instead of showing compassion by giving aid to those in need, people can show compassion by voting for political leaders who promise to introduce social programs which will aid the needy. Instead of showing integrity by supporting the causes in which they believe, they can show integrity by acting politically to promote those causes. So why does society need to leave room for virtuous philanthropic activities and encourage their performance by tax benefits? I think that there is a good answer to this challenge. In truth, the political decision-making process of a society is something very alien to most citizens. For better or for worse, if the opportunity to display the various virtues is to be a real opportunity for most, it will have to be because the state has allowed ample space for private philanthropy and has actively encouraged it. We may need to make sure by direct state action that the most important needs are covered, but we must also leave important space for private philanthropy.

Will private philanthropic activities be virtuous if they are motivated by favorable tax treatment? Won't they simply turn into selfish actions? I think that this final objection reflects a major confusion. Nobody can be selfishly motivated to make philanthropic gifts simply by virtue of the fact that we have lowered the burden of doing so. There must be an independent motivation for making the gift. The tax treatment can, at best, lessen the burden, thereby encouraging people to behave virtuously.

The skeptics have certainly raised serious questions about the role of private philanthropy in a free and democratic society. We have seen, however, that there are three ways in which those questions can be met.

Philosophy, Rice University and Center for Ethics, Baylor College of Medicine

MORAL PLURALISM AND PHILANTHROPY

By David Sidorsky

The idea of moral pluralism generates a dilemma for the practice of philanthropy. Characteristically, the practice of philanthropy assumes unity, coherence, or convergence among the diverse virtues and moral aims that it pursues. In the philanthropic tradition, it is recognized that the goals of a particular philanthropy will vary. Yet, if these are sincere expressions of the philanthropic will, each represents some portion of the manifold activity of "doing good" according to particularized choice or style. The relevant analogy should be drawn to the slogan of "giving to the college of your choice" or to worship of the one god in your own way, where the plurality of expression is not only consistent with the residual value of education or of religion, but articulates the pragmatic way to realize the underlying values of a pluralistic society.

Historically, this reflects the place of a unifying religious vision of the nature of the good or of a secular conception of a public philosophy which recognized the common good. Even etymologically, the love of mankind suggests a single passion that is directed beneficently to the shared values of mankind.

The theory and practice of contemporary philanthropy is necessarily pluralistic, however, and it reflects the range of decisions by individuals with different interests and values in a pluralist, democratic society. The legitimized and recognized range of philanthropies in modern societies demonstrates divergent and even conflicting perceptions of the common good or the public interest.

Thus, the range of philanthropies includes support for bird watching and for business opportunities of minorities, which may require some decisions on "comparable worth" and competitive allocation of resources. It also includes support for environmentalism and for economic development in public policy, which may involve latent conflict. More significantly, it can include support for one kind of environmental solution that calls for the restriction of nuclear energy, and support for a certain kind of economic development that requires eliminating the restriction of nuclear energy.

The tension and possibility of conflict is apparent. It suggests the formal dilemma: if philanthropic plurality is recognized, then the pursuit of some goals which could negate others is appropriate. Hence, the common good will not be served. If service to a common good is a condition of philanthropic legitimacy, then some procedure for establishing a moral hierarchy and the ordering of priorities for the exclusion of conflict would be required.

The emergence of this dilemma might be blocked by a closer examination of the nature of pluralism. This is the approach of the first part of this paper. Alternatively, methods for resolving the dilemma through the integration of a plurality of virtues with the idea of the common good can be suggested. The elucidation of some of the methods used for this purpose that derive from Aristotle and the classical moral tradition is the program of the second part of this paper.

If the dilemma is not resolved, then a realistic recognition of the fact that some philanthropic activity will be harmful emerges. The recognition of this commonplace is not paradoxical, for unless philanthropic activities could cause harm, there would be no point in praising the wise and judicious exercise of philanthropic intentions.

I. The Models of Pluralism

One way to foreclose the dilemma is to examine how pluralism could be compatible with the idea of a common good. This compatibility is claimed in many forms of pluralism, including political pluralism in a democratic society, pluralism of inquiry in the universities, religious pluralism in a secular or tolerant society, pluralism of tastes in cultural expression, and even economic pluralism in a free marketplace. In each of these cases, without an accepted moral hierarchy or an explicit public philosophy, there is a rationale for the view that pluralism is consistent with the common good. Accordingly, one beginning for the examination of moral pluralism in philanthropy is to test the difference between the condition of philanthropy and these other forms of pluralism.

1. Political Pluralism and the Visible Hand

A. The Negotiation of Consent
The plural interest group theory of democratic political process requires the negotiation of consent among all the organized groups in a society. The main criterion for the validity of political decisions is not their objective adequacy as a political solution to the political problems of the society, but that they are the true outcomes of the consensual process. This process involves elections in which the representatives are to be accepted by the community if they win the majority of the votes cast, not on the basis of the validity or truth of their platforms. It necessarily involves bargaining among elected representatives who must be amenable to pressure or persuasion

exercised by various special interest groups that are not organized for the sake of the common good. To a significant degree, the validity of the process depends upon the ability of each group to assert its interests in the course of the decision-making process. The outcome of the negotiation of consent then articulates a weighted representation of the interest groups of the society.

On this model, the previously unorganized or under-represented groups must be able to become participants in the process. The model assumes that the participation of such groups, even if they engender new sources of conflict or tension, is required in order to achieve integration and consensus. The value assumption is that an effective and good political society is one in which no interest group is repressed or driven underground but, rather, all potential interest groups find ways of asserting their interests. Accordingly, the maximization of pluralism is a major value in the political mode.

The resulting proliferation of plural interest groups in a democracy bears some measure of analogy to moral pluralism in philanthropy with its funding of innovative or previously unrecognized groups or programs. The distinctive difference, however, is that the political process assumes and requires mechanisms for negotiation of consent which serve to "close" the issue. What is also significant is that decisions based on election results are part of this "closure" in the negotiation of consent, either through distribution of offices according to election outcomes or by adoption of legislation through voting by representatives.

There is an element of analogy between moral pluralism in philanthropy and political pluralism. Decisions by budgetary allocation may involve reaching a consensus, often through public debate and media agenda setting in the philanthropic as in the political sphere. There is not and ought not to be a mechanism that fulfills for philanthropies the closure role in the political process of negotiation of consent among the parties and groups in competition.

A partial probing of some recent issues that test the boundaries of philanthropic pluralism may illustrate the patterns of resemblance and difference between political pluralism and moral pluralism in philanthropy. Philanthropic grants to an organization of antinuclear physicians that includes Soviet and American doctors supports a particular set of values whose pursuit is recognized and permissible within American law. Simultaneous support for other medical organizations whose purpose is to boycott Soviet-American medical cooperation or scientific exchange until the practice of psychiatric detention of Soviet dissidents is halted is also a permissible expression of American values. It may even be that in some broad process of communal awareness, the two instruments of philanthropy are coherent. Simultaneous support for public forums that present the views of a committee of Soviet and American physicians, which includes a member of the Central Committee of the Communist Party of the Soviet Union, as a "front" or "agit-prop" organization might also be construed as a further contribution to the formation of awareness in the area. The coherence of these actions would be problematic, but each can be justified as part of a philanthropic effort, so that this could be a contribution to a complex common good. A governmental program that would support these three initiatives would probably be judged, however, to be incoherent or an evasion of moral responsibility.

The extension of the pluralist range in a similar but more immediate type of policy action sharpens the point. Philanthropic support of humanitarian assistance for the Sandinista government in Nicaragua and for the groups fighting to overthrow the Sandinista regime can both be justified in moral terms by their supporters. The idea that fund-raising drives should escalate the total gift – the United Way slogan could urge giving to the freedom fighter of your choice – would, however, be self-defeating for the moral purpose of both sides. Within the political process, there are methods provided by governmental budgetary decision making for excluding or limiting one or the other form of humanitarian assistance. The process of philanthropic pluralism provides no mechanism for this kind of exclusion except the bar against illegal action. The difference suggests that the justification of pluralism in philanthropy rests on grounds that are different from the justification of pluralism in the political process.

B. A Note on Philanthropic Agencies and the Group Interest Model

The distinction between moral pluralism in philanthropy and political pluralism may be relevant also to the tensions that are present when philanthropic approaches enter into an interest-group process. An area for examination would be the ways in which some philanthropic foundations functioned in the emergence and proliferation of community or ethnic interest groups in the "War on Poverty" agenda in the late 1960s.

As previously noted, the assumption of a plural interest political model is that every potential group interest should be articulated in the decision-making process. Accordingly, philanthropic actions in support of the historically deprived or unrecognized constituencies or interests involved the funding of new interest groups. This was also justified on the assumption that such groups had been excluded from a participatory role in the society. Their organization, initially as "venting" or grievance groups and, subsequently, as agents in the decision-making process, would channel energies away from violent expression, riots, or revolt, and into the constructive avenues of the democratic process. In pursuit of this pluralism, specialized experts in community organization, including advocacy planning in housing, consumer advocacy, experts in confrontational organization tactics, and legal advocacy groups, received philanthropic support.

The mechanisms of negotiation of consent in community participation forums were to be applied to issues which had traditionally been part of a more limited governmental decision making, from site selection in housing to budgets for school programs. Consequently, some of the traditional ethnic, institutional, or political constituencies were challenged by the new advocacy groups.

In the process of negotiation of consent among the expanded plural groups, some of the traditional ethnic constituencies were represented by philanthropic agencies, professional or voluntary. These agencies had historically related to the newly organized groups as patrons or supporters. Accordingly, they did not function as interest groups asserting the interests of their constituencies in a plural political process.

Virtually systemically, the interests of the constituency groups that were represented by philanthropic bodies were neglected. The common sense of the situation is apparent. If in a negotiating framework each group asserts its interests while some groups pursue their sense of the common good, the inevitable compromises will be made at the expense of those groups whose interests have not been defended.

The moral evaluation of such an outcome is ambiguous. It can be argued that the outcome reflects the interests that were articulated in the process in an optimal or reasonable way. Those groups which were represented by philanthropic groups had an interest in the support of other values, rather than the more traditional interests of their constituency. These values could be the improvement of their moral self-image, their special interest in what is perceived as moral progress, or even their interest in co-optation.

It could be argued, on the other hand, that the outcome represents a distortion of the political process model. The analogy would be an advocacy trial system in which the advocate for one of the parties construes his role as a philanthropic interest in the common good, rather than a narrow defense of his client in an adversarial contest. The moral force of this criticism is that the philanthropic advocate has sacrificed his constituency's interests, not his own.

The neglect of the representation of traditional interest groups for the sake of newly organized groups, whose numbers are strengthened by philanthropic transfusion, would result in long-term deleterious consequences on the assumption of the political process model that the outcome of the process is the common good. This model is open to the challenge that it ought not to block philanthropic groups pursuing the common good in conflict-of-interest situations. One resolution could be an objective measure, if it were achievable by a moral or historical analysis, of the adequacy of the alternative approaches used in these circumstances. This inquiry cannot be pursued in the present context. The relevance of the illustration is the distinction between philanthropic pluralism and political pluralism, so that the processes or justification of political pluralism cannot be directly transposed to philanthropic pluralism.

2. Pluralism and Academic Freedom

Academic freedom assumes pluralism, both in the range of points of view toward subjects at issue and in the diversity of faculty or guests presenting information on these subjects that will be permitted or encouraged by the university. The concomitant assumption is that the university or the faculty in its *corporate* or *institutional* role will not be a participant in political decision making. Accordingly, there is a significant difference between the pluralist model of the university in its concern for academic freedom and the political model of philanthropic pluralism. The role of the philanthropic foundation or agency may be support or advocacy of a particular approach to the subject. A "pluralist" effort to support financially or to advocate politically conflicting or competing actions could be incoherent or self-defeating.

There is some justification for weakening the distinction between academic pluralism and the moral pluralism of philanthropy. Freedom of inquiry does not exclude particular institutions from setting limitations on plural views in a manner analogous to a philanthropic foundation defining its purposes and areas of support. The university is not required to strive for a complete representation of all points of view. The University of Chicago, for example, is identified with a particular approach to economic and legal theory which contrasts with that of Harvard. Apart from this narrowing of the range of perspectives, there are a number of ways legitimized by institutional practice in which unintended selectivity or constraints emerge. The University of Chicago economist Von Hayek believed that his best conservative students went into banking and his best liberal students chose university teaching. Such a narrowing of pluralism is not proof of a breakdown of academic freedom.

One criterion would be discrimination in hiring against persons of differing points of view on other grounds than the recognized scholarly or academic criteria. If this test is met, then presumably a range of opinions will emerge of sufficient plurality throughout the universities so that the free forum of ideas persists.

It can be argued that the restriction against discriminatory exclusion on grounds of ideological or political opinion is insufficient. The risk of conformity through politicization of the university, in this view, requires affirmative action in support of the recruitment or cultivation of dissenting points of view. For example, it would not suffice that the professors at the university's school of engineering are virtually unanimous in their support of nuclear energy while the professors at the same university's school of journalism are virtually unanimous in opposition. Pluralism could require that some anti-nuclear engineers be hired while some pronuclear energy journalists be created. The operative conception of academic pluralism does not mandate any minimum representation or quota distribution of nonconformist opinion. There is statistical evidence of limitation of pluralism by a kind of professional deformation in the Academy. The continuing assumption has been that a nondiscriminatory marketplace of competition among academic talent will generate a sufficiently plural range of opinion.

University actions as a corporate body in the advocacy of political views presumably have a negative impact on academic pluralism. Such advocacy probably tends to drive dissenting opinion underground even when it does not stifle all expression of dissenting opinion. The decision by a university board of trustees to divest, accompanied by a degree of student coercion, does not necessarily result in the silencing of those professors in the university who believe in alternative approaches in human rights policy. Those who would argue for nonintervention in the affairs of a sovereign state, human rights action only through international agencies, quiet diplomacy or constructive engagement, or strategies of linkage through economic leverage can pursue these arguments after a divestment decision has been made. The sustaining of pluralism required for academic freedom is probably made more difficult, however, by corporate action of the university.

Despite the differentiating commitment to "doing good" rather than to freedom of inquiry, a philanthropic foundation can and often does support a pluralist range of studies or grants for action on controversial subjects. An orientation toward problem solving may even mandate the funding of a variety of approaches, some of which are in conflict.

Despite the qualifications upon the distinction between moral pluralism in philanthropy and pluralism of inquiry in the university, the force of the distinction remains. The university is the sole institution dedicated primarily to freedom of inquiry. Its distinctive primary role permits its legitimate insulation from political or other pressures from diverse constituencies or advocacy groups upon its freedom to pursue plural lines of inquiry or to employ a broad and diverse faculty. The value of the results of its inquiry are, to a degree, dependent upon the freedom of inquiry. As part of the implementation of its primary purpose, the university commitment to nonpoliticization and pluralism of inquiry is required. While a philanthropic institution is required to avoid political partisanship, the terms of its social contract with the public are different from the university. Accordingly, the moral pluralism of philanthropy does not require the degree of value neutrality in inquiry or the preservation of the pluralism of approaches required for academic freedom.

3. Religious Pluralism and Pluralism of Tastes

There is a traditional connection between the view of philanthropy as the pursuit of a coherent set of moral goals and religious morality. Accordingly, one avenue for the exploration of moral pluralism in contemporary philanthropy would be the examination of religious pluralism. The acceptance of religious differences that characterized religious reform and religious pluralism suggests patterns of symmetry to the pluralism of moral goals and readiness for innovation and experiment that emerged in philanthropic pluralism.

There are some aspects of religious pluralism that would justify the use of this symmetry, both on the historical record and in the conceptual framework. This would apply where pluralism involved going beyond the idea of *coexistence* of the "self" and the "other," to the *legitimization* of the existence of the "other." Even more, pluralism can require that one group's recognition of the "other" be carried out in terms of the other's self-definition and self-perception. This requirement generates patterns of moral conflict for religious pluralism similar to the dilemmas of philanthropic pluralism.

To a significant degree, however, the justification of religious pluralism has not required any such severe form of pluralism. Historically, many of the arguments for religious pluralism were morally prudential, appealing to the high moral and pragmatic costs of religious coercion and to the minimal moral or practical value of coerced conversion. Within a coherent hierarchy of moral values held by an institutional religion that does not accept an indifferent religious pluralism, the benefit of religious conformism may be outweighed by the costs of attaining such unity or conformism in a pluralist society.

The pattern of moral argument that is used for the justification of religious pluralism confirms the difference between moral pluralism in philanthropy and religious pluralism. Characteristically, the justification for religious tolerance was the similarity of value commitment in the other religion that deserved to be tolerated. In that sense, pluralism required the relegation to insignificance of such "outward" or secondary aspects of religion as ritual, language, and form and style of worship, and appropriate appreciation of the "inward" or major substance of moral value. In the parable of Lessing's play *Nathan the Wise*, which is paradigmatic for religious tolerance in the Enlightenment, the authentic magical ring transmitted over generations can only be distinguished from the counterfeit ring by its *moral* powers. All major religions share, in this view, the *core* of ethical culture.

The distinction emerges clearly in the secularization of contemporary philanthropy. The implicit assumption was that religion set plural philanthropic activities within a hierarchical value structure. Secular moral pluralism cannot assume the preestablished harmony of a philanthropic hierarchy.

An alternative contemporary interpretation of religious pluralism also does not lead toward moral pluralism in philanthropy. Religious pluralism has been justified on the ground that all religious claims and practices are conventional matters of taste. The corollary is that there is no dispute about tastes. In its most general form, this would justify a plurality of tastes without any moral hierarchy or plurality.

While there may be some cases in which moral pluralism in philanthropy is an acceptance of a principle of plenitude for the variety of tastes, the governing assumption would be that some set of moral goods is being fulfilled. A justification of philanthropic purposes on the ground of expression of diversity or plurality of taste would presumably require some reason why such diversity or plurality should be encouraged. This justification would itself not be a matter of taste, but would require some element of moral purpose.

A philanthropy which supports a range of cultural enterprises, including works of high culture and presumably good taste, as well as works of mass culture, pop culture, and even "debased" taste, can justify this pluralism on a range of implicit moral values. The support for various forms of musical activity, for example, can be based on different moral reasons. Apart from the possible moral worth of self-expression by any group of persons, moral values being supported include the release of repression, the channeling of potentially destructive energy, the sublimation or purging of a potential for violence through an artistic event, and the need for human communion in a contemporary illusory mode of artistic endeavor.

Similarly, the support for works of high culture or artistic excellence need not be justified in terms of plurality of taste, whether arbitrary or objective. There are diverse moral values implicit in such support. These range from the fact that some works enhance the quality of life to the satisfactions that are derived from the ritualistic performance of the conventions of elitist culture. These values can be supported by a philanthropic institution without acceptance or denial of the individual tastes within the plurality. The same would not apply to conflicting moral choices, even if they are described as issues of taste. The problem for moral pluralism, accordingly, is not modeled on the plurality of tastes. Moral pluralism in philanthropy confronts moral conflict and moral coherence in terms that are different from its openness to diversity of taste. Thus, moral pluralism in philanthropy does not have access to the traditional moral hierarchy which was implicit in religious pluralism, nor can it be based upon the irrelevance of morality which may be legitimate for the diversity of aesthetic tastes.

4. Economic Pluralism and the Invisible Hand

The significant difference between the moral pluralism of philanthropy and the economic pluralism ascribed to free market economics is elucidated by the metaphor of the invisible hand. The free market, like the pluralist political process, assumes relative ease of access by all participants to the economic marketplace, whether as workers, producers, investors, or consumers. Unlike the pluralist political model, there is no negotiating of consent among these participants. On the economic model, free-market mechanisms serve to integrate the individual assertion of interests into an optimal allocation of resources, an optimal setting of the price of labor, capital, or goods. Although this allocation of resources is optimal and therefore ultimately beneficial to all members of the economic society, it is not necessarily philanthropic. It involves, as a matter of course, such non-philanthropic action as creative destruction through the discipline of bankruptcy or of unemployment in order to arrive at optimal allocation of resources.

There is no such invisible hand among the plural aims of philanthropic institutions. Counterproductive philanthropic actions will not result in philanthropic bankruptcy by the forum of foundations, just as wise and beneficent philanthropy need not achieve recognition and incentive rewards within that forum. The contrast can be particularized through noting the differences between the moral goods achieved and the economic strategies required in the operation of Standard Oil, U.S. Steel, and Ford Motors, and the Rockefeller, Carnegie, and Ford Foundations. Whatever the metaphorical character of the invisible hand, the satisfaction of the interests of the corporation's stockholders through legal means which bring about a reduction of the activities of competing corporations is appropriate. It is difficult to construe as legitimate philanthropic activity which results in the beneficial elimination of a competing foundation. The reason is presumably the assumption of an invisible hand in corporate competition and the absence of such a mechanism for selection among philanthropies in any marketplace of Foundations.

5. The Special Character of Moral Pluralism

This review of some variant forms of pluralism has suggested that in each of them, there is a recognized mechanism for reconciling the pluralist values within the model with an interpretation of the common good. As I noted, political pluralism posits the negotiation of consent among competing interest groups as itself a "process equivalent" of the common good. Similarly, a pluralist model of freedom of inquiry in the university assumes that the conditions that permit freedom are the unique value, even if – or partly because – they exclude any special results in social policy. Religious pluralism is justified, in significant measure, by the recognition that it permits diverse groups to pursue underlying and shared moral values in their own ways. Analogously, advocacy of a plurality of tastes may represent, in moral terms, a unified set of underlying moral values, such as tolerance and self-expression. The pluralism of the free, egoistic, and competitive marketplace assumes that social benefits in economic terms are the outcome of the market activity.

No similar mechanism for reconciling the plural aims and values of philanthropy with its sense of the common good was uncovered. This suggests that moral pluralism in philanthropy faces a dilemma which can be resolved in either of two ways. One direction would be to attempt to reconstruct the traditional idea of the public philosophy. This may involve some constraints on the range of plurality for the sake of a more integrative vision of the common good. The other direction would be to pursue a plurality of goals in a diverse and fragmented society. This pursuit involves the recognition of the reality of conflict among the plurality of philanthropic ideals.

II. Moral Pluralism and the Common Good: Three Ways of Resolving the Dilemma

The dilemma of the plurality of moral goods and the search for a common good that is implicit in the practice of contemporary philanthropy can be rooted in the tradition of ethical inquiry. Probably the classical locus for the question is Aristotle's effort to expand the plurality of the virtues in a manner consistent with the univocal interpretation of happiness or the good life. In developing the arguments for this resolution of the dilemma, Aristotle provides three different patterns of argument. These patterns can serve as the basis for an examination of strategies for eliminating or reducing the tension between moral pluralism and the common good.

The Aristotelian arguments derive from a different set of problems. Aristotle inherited the debate between Plato and the Sophists as to whether the virtues were one or many. In that debate, a canonical short list of virtues – wisdom, courage, justice, temperance in the *Republic*, conjoined with holiness in the *Protagoras* – are analyzed in terms of their reducibility, similarity, or shared properties. Plato's demonstration that these virtues have a common element was connected to his more general view that the plurality of moral virtues presupposes the existence of an idea of the good.

Apart from a number of theoretical considerations, the pragmatic criterion suggested by Aristotle that is most relevant to the present problem is that the demonstration of the existence of the single or common good must be related and useful to decisions about better or worse policies or actions in practice. The assertion of a public philosophy or of a vision of the good which would not serve to guide policy on the plural issues would become an empty, formulaic obeisance.

Aristotle's concern over the applicability of the idea of the common good has special force in light of his own recognition of a plurality of virtues distinct from the four or five cardinal virtues. According to Aristotle, for any human activity that involves rational decision making, there is the possibility of an excessive, deficient, or appropriate pattern of human habit or response. Human virtues or excellences are identified with the appropriate dispositions for action in the entire range of human activities.

Political virtue or virtue in human action can thus not be encapsulated in the primary virtues. If philanthropic giving, for example, is an area of human activity that generates a continuum of responses, the appropriate generosity or liberality comes between a deficient niggardliness and an exhibitionistic or unsustainable prodigality. If recent political experience suggests novel political responses to terrorist outrage, there is the morally appropriate anger which is located between passivity and rage. The list of virtues is not infinite, but its length extends to the variety of social contexts and the extensive pluralism of the descriptive or evaluative vocabulary of human behavior.

There is a question of interpretation concerning whether Aristotle continues the Platonic tradition of the small number of primary virtues or reverts to the pre-Socratic method of effectively defining the virtues by listing the different kinds of excellence that emerge in different contexts. (As Eliot wrote: "Do not ask what is it. Let us go and pay a visit.") In any event, the post-Aristotelian tradition retained an emphasis upon a selected group of virtues deemed to be consistent with the recognition of moral pluralism and with the common good.

Thus, Philippa Foot has written on the significance of that tradition for contemporary concerns in the following way:

> [I]t is best when considering the virtues and vices to go back to Aristotle and Aquinas. . . . It is certain, in any case, that the most systematic account is found in Aristotle. . . .
>
> There is, however, one minor obstacle to be overcome when one goes back to Aristotle and Aquinas for help in constructing a theory of virtues, namely a lack of coincidence between their terminology and our own. . . . 'The virtues' to us are the moral virtues, whereas *arete* and *virtus* refer also to arts, and even to excellences of the speculative intellect. . . . For us, there are four cardinal moral virtues: courage, temperance, wisdom and justice. . . . Nobody can get on well if he lacks courage, and does not have some measure of temperance and wisdom, while communities where justice and

charity are lacking are apt to be wretched places to live as Russia was under Stalinist terror, or Sicily under the Mafia. . . .[1]

It is noteworthy how the contemporary examples seem to go beyond the claim that the cardinal virtues for us are those four which Plato sought to establish in his republic. This point is recognized by Philippa Foot at least in part, for she notes that charity is lacking in Soviet Russia under Stalin, or in Sicily. The obvious suggestion is that it was a measure of tolerance or respect for the rights of others, or some aspect of political virtue related to freedom that would ordinarily come to mind as the virtue needed under Stalin.

There are several other vices and correlative virtues that would emerge in any contemporary moral assessment of "Stalinist" rule or "Mafia" practice, and – except by antecedent invocation – these would not coincide with wisdom, courage, justice, and temperance, or with their denial.

In the case of Stalin, there is the question of moral dogmatism becoming an instrument of manipulation, followed by a ruthless and suspicious fanaticism. The Aristotelian paradigm suggests ways in which these excessive and deficient tendencies could be characterized with reference to their appropriate mean. The moral vocabulary is contextual and plural, including trust as opposed to suspiciousness; honesty or openness in dealings as opposed to secrecy, duplicity, or treachery; and a sense of limits which is not identical with the Greek idea of temperance. In the case of a culture of Mafiosi, one relevant Aristotelian move would be the question of the appropriate measure of "manliness." Prosper Merimee, in *Mateo Falcone*, has sketched the classical Corsican code of honor in his story in which the father kills his beloved son for informing to the authorities on a fugitive from justice. A faulty interpretation of machismo is, of course, not the only relevant component in a moral assessment which involves a complex set of social virtues and vices.

The significant utilization of Aristotle for the present context, however, is not his introduction of moral pluralism. A directory of philanthropic foundations provides an abundant list of the variety of virtues, whether of morality, art, or intellect, which should be supported or sustained. Aristotle's ethical writings provide, as noted, three ways in which a plurality of goods are related to the idea of the common good.

The first is the claim that a political process involving the discussion and determination of the citizens of the polis provides a way of ranking moral ends and developing the required moral hierarchy. The second is the claim

---

[1] Philippa Foot, "Virtues and Vices," *Virtues and Vices and Other Essays in Moral Philosophy* (Oxford: Basil Blackwell, 1978), p. 2.

that an understanding of the unique biological function of the human species provides the necessary basis for deriving the goods or ends of man. The account of man's place in the scale of nature leads to an understanding of the primary values of mankind, as distinct from mankind's secondary or less important values, or from the unique values of other forms of life. The third claim is that the identification of commonly accepted moral virtues is possible through the convergence of judgment by men of practical reason and prudence.

Each of these three methods indicates a *partial* resolution of the dilemma of moral pluralism in philanthropy and the pursuit of the common good. The examination of their success as well as of their inadequacy can clarify the contemporary dilemma.

1. Political Process and Moral Hierarchy

Despite the difficulties in the application of a political process of negotiation of consent to the moral pluralism of the community in philanthropy that have been previously sketched, political decision making sets the limits on the framework of moral pluralism in philanthropy. Thus, the American government decided that orgone boxes were fraudulent ways to seek to help troubled persons regardless of the eminence of their psychiatrist sponsors, or that tax-exempt philanthropic agencies cannot be lobbies for foreign governments, even for beneficent purposes. These and many similar decisions by government that draw the lines of philanthropic pursuits leave open a framework for the kind of moral pluralism that generates conflict on what is the common good and permits opposing policies for the realization of the perceived good.

A possible analogy to the conception of an Aristotelian political process, in which communication among the citizens in a public forum sets a hierarchy of values, may exist within the community of major institutionalized philanthropic agencies. The empirical exploration of this analogy would be relevant to the ways of reconciling moral pluralism with an idea of the common good. There is, however, significant difference between the rationality of political decision making for Aristotle and contemporary practice, with implication for the plurality of philanthropic goals in contemporary society. To a greater degree than in the classical or medieval tradition, there is not a univocal description of complex or contested social events that is shared by the community.

Accordingly, the political problem in setting up a moral hierarchy or in determining the best policy within a continuum cannot be described in the Aristotelian terms of drawing the line between the excessive and the deficient norm or between the higher and lower actualization of a potential good. Disagreement by morally sensitive and well-informed persons is not relegated to debate on borderline issues, but is polarized.

At the risk of using illustrative material that is too controversial and political for the logical demonstration, the issues that dominated moral debate in the past decade can be cited to document the equivocal interpretation and perception of contemporary social reality. Philanthropic support for the "peace" movement during the war in Vietnam relied significantly on an interpretation of the nature of that war. It was perceived as a civil war within Vietnam, so that American involvement was an illegitimate intervention that violated the national self-determination of the Vietnamese people. Philanthropic support for American intervention relied on an alternative perception of the war. It was a war of aggression by one part of a divided nation against the other, similar to the invasion by North Korea of South Korea, or a hypothetical invasion by East Germany of West Germany. For the United States to withdraw under these circumstances would have been to abandon a beleaguered ally. Such an abandonment leads to tragic human consequences as well as to deleterious security consequences with long-range implications for the community.

The relevant problem for philanthropy is not the adjudication of this issue. The point is that the competing perceptions provide strong moral justification for each of the views that are in conflict. The values to which each party of the debate appeals, like self-determination or resistance to aggression, are shared values that appear on the support list of the contending philanthropies. Yet, presumably, no common good would emerge in increasing support to each.

Even when an issue achieves a measure of political consensus, there are unresolved competing interpretations of the social reality. By the denouement of Watergate, there had been a measure of political consensus. Philanthropic support for activities aimed at minimizing political corruption or abuse of office proliferated, based on the assumption that Watergate represented such a moral agenda.

One alternative interpretation is that Watergate was a media coup in which a number of events that have long characterized American politics, like finding out sensitive information about political opponents, were highlighted by the agenda-setting powers of the electronic media. As a result, in an alliance with Congress, the traditional power of the Presidency was limited with catastrophic consequences for American foreign policy. The widespread philanthropic activities to develop standards of accountability for the media or to assist watchdog groups that examine the accuracy of the media reflect, at least in part, this interpretation. Thus, even the existence of a widely shared political consensus should not exclude philanthropic support for the minority or revisionist view.

It can be argued that the support for plural perspectives on contemporary social reality, even when they are in conflict, will ultimately enhance the common good. Such an argument (that would probably be persuasive for some cases of conflict and not plausible for others) would, in any event, go beyond the conception of any political process that can provide a moral hierarchy for the compelling plurality of values.

2. The Primary Ends of Man as the Moral Arbiter of Philanthropy

The second device for reconciling the plurality of virtues that are recognized with the idea of the common good is the use of the biological function of man. Many of the virtues appeal to the excellences of a person in a social role as parent, soldier, worker, entrepreneur, or artist. The analysis of the biological function of mankind would then provide the common residue of these social roles, the end of man *qua* man.

When that end is interpreted as happiness or the good life, there remain the competing perceptions of happiness. Aristotle suggests, for example, that happiness is identified with victory by the general, with wealth by the entrepreneur, and with pleasure by the bon vivant. Yet, these goods can be subsumed under the more inclusive sense of happiness for man *qua* man.

The application of this Aristotelian approach to the dilemma of moral pluralism in philanthropy suggests a line of resolution. In light of the preceding comment on the equivocal nature of social perceptions, one strategy would be to focus on the shared goods that seem most necessary to all persons. The candidates in terms of health, food, shelter, and other recognized minimal conditions for human life are familiar beneficiaries of philanthropic effort. These would appear to be neutral, that is, not equivocally perceived. So, while individual philanthropies would pursue what could be recognized as "private" moral agendas, the major "public" agenda would relate to these core values derived from the shared biological needs of the human species.

It is ironic, and may be instructive, to note how opposed this result would be to the conclusion that Aristotle derived. For the needs of food, health, or growth are those that human beings share with the plants and animals of the world. The unique biological role or end of the human species is connected with its rationality. So, on this ground, foundation support should flow to philosophers, astronomers, musicians, mathematicians, and others who express or participate in the distinctive biological potentialities of the human species, even if their numbers are a statistical fraction of the population.

Whether this interpretation is accepted or not, it suggests that the criterion that the end or good is the actualization of the potentialities of being a human being will not serve as a public philosophy for contemporary philanthropy. Plural and competing ends can be reasserted in ways which make them fundamental to human fulfillment of function.

Concentrating upon the recognized biological necessities cannot eliminate the context-related conflict. It may be that in a critical period, as in a famine situation, contextual considerations become secondary. Yet, the food policy of philanthropic agencies to countries like Ethiopia or India, for the long run, cannot avoid contested questions. The use by the Ethiopian government of food policy as an instrument of population relocation to crush political dissent can be overridden, but it cannot be avoided by stressing the needs of the suffering persons. The export of free wheat to a famine-threatened country cannot overlook the import of costly tanks by the same country at the same time. The potential harm to indigenous farming by free or low-cost food imports cannot be dismissed because of the importance of short-term improvement in nutrition in a developing country. Similar issues will arise in medical care, housing policy, or other "biologically-related" candidates for a criterion of the common good. That the justification in theory for a politically neutral, in one sense even "value-neutral," philanthropy is open to criticism because of nonneutral contexts of application and consequences has long been recognized. It remains significant that one possibility for the reconciliation of moral pluralism with an idea of the common good has been the perennial option to direct philanthropy into such traditional goals as those which relate to minimal human needs. Similarly, this analysis leads to a restoration of emphasis on support of historically sanctioned "neutral" institutions like education or religion.

3. Convergence as Confirmation or Trendiness

The identification of moral virtue in situations of disagreement, for Aristotle, depends upon the possibility of a convergence of judgment by prudent persons who can exercise practical reason. This criterion of convergence has been used in analogous ways in modern contexts. In particular, the Deweyan social ethic that had been so influential in American culture and society invoked the conception of convergence through the application of critical intelligence or scientific method.

The argument did not rest on Aristotle's confidence in human reason as much as in confidence in the methods of science. The adoption of scientific method in the natural sciences seemed to assure convergence. By a commitment to the experimental method of inquiry, scientists could be confident that the views that gained acceptance in the contemporary period were superior to those of the past and would be transcended in the future only for valid reasons. Even when the criticisms, developed by Kuhn and others, of this confidence in convergence are recognized, as a practical matter the commitment to convergence within the domain of the sciences continues.

On the Deweyan reinterpretation of Aristotelian naturalism in ethics, scientific method provides the basis for convergence on moral issues. The social sciences provide the methods for investigation into the moral questions of social practice. What is required is the willingness to apply experimental methods of inquiry to moral and social issues.

Moral pluralism in philanthropy provides a test of the argument for scientific convergence on moral issues through the exercise of practical reason or the application of experimental method in the social sciences. The claim by a philanthropic institution that its moral aims are consistent with the common good because they are the product of social scientific inquiry would probably generate a measure of skepticism.

One of the more generalized forms of that skepticism is the argument that the convergence of social scientific inquiry represents a phenomenon more closely resembling the adoption of a trend in fashion than the presumably progressive and self-correcting method of scientific inquiry. In one interpretation, the hypothesis is advanced that this "trendiness" within the social sciences derives from the ideological bias of its practitioners, who are members of a "New Class." In this interpretation, the New Class represents an adversarial group that is opposed to the traditional institutions of American family and business culture. The mutually reinforcing activities of the New Class explain why the conclusions of social science seem to confirm the views that are congenial to the dominant groups within the New Class. These are the faculties of major universities, writers and editors of the major media of communications, and, to a degree, the executives of philanthropic foundations.

The establishment or rejection of the "New Class" interpretation is outside the frame of reference of the current discussion. The relevance of that interpretation is that it provides one possible account of convergence which subverts the Aristotelian model. In the traditional version, the problem of circularity was recognized: the criterion for a person who possesses "practical reason" is not independent of the judgment or acceptance of other persons who are alleged to have "practical reason." Accordingly, the process of convergence can represent, as noted, the ways in which a fashion, style, or trend achieves pervasive temporary dominance before being displaced by another. It can also represent a cumulative tendency toward a mistaken or false view.

Rousseau used an analogue of the method of convergence to permit the transition from the "will of the majority," which can err, to the "general will," which is expressive of the common good. Yet, the required assumption for that convergence is that each individual within the majority is more likely to be right about his own interests than to be mistaken. If contrarian models of economic forecasting, for example, on the assumption that the individuals in the community were more likely to be wrong, even by a margin of 51%, then the convergent trend line would be wrong by a margin of 79%. The correct approach when faced with a convergent trend would then be to adopt a contrary strategy toward the trend.

The application of the argument to the philanthropic context could require that philanthropic agencies consider the policy recommendations accepted by the majority of social scientists to have a high probability of being counterproductive. It could then require that philanthropic agencies consider the convergence of views of their staffs to be a kind of index signaling the adoption of contrary policies. The relevance of the argument does not, however, reside in these *jeux d'esprit*. It serves to establish that the convergence toward a consensus does not necessarily reflect the integration of the plural values and interests of the community.

There are other paradigms in the tradition of ethical inquiry for reconciling the diversity of particular moral prizings and appraisals with a conception of the common good. Yet, conjoined with the earlier exercise of showing how difficult the mechanisms of such a reconciliation are compared with other forms of pluralism, the examination of these three patterns lends additional support for a conclusion. The conclusion could be buttressed by both historical argument and empirical evidence. It would seem to follow that if so many diverse persons and agencies seek to do good by supporting a multiplicity of projects and activities, some of these will embody conflicting aims and realizations. Accordingly, the moral pluralism of philanthropy would not share or reflect a common good. The truistic summary of the matter is that sometimes the intention to do good results in evil.

III. Conclusion: The "Paradox" of Moral Pluralism in Philanthropy

The truistic character of the claim that a morally pluralistic set of philanthropic institutions shares no substantive idea of the common good does not deny the importance of that claim. The preceding review of some of the arguments that exhibit the difficulties in developing formulae or mechanisms of such reconciliation serves to underscore the risks of philanthropic commitment. Even some foundations and institutions that are carefully structured and well staffed for the sake of doing some portion of the common good will not realize this intention. There are systemic reasons why they will do some harm.

The conclusion has an air of paradox. If doing harm is inevitable for the set of institutions whose purpose is solely the doing of good, then some new framework seems to be required. The suggestion of a paradox is, however, misleading. It is instructive to note its similarity to the claim that there is a "paradox of democracy."

According to the construction of that paradox, voters in a democracy express their preference for policies or representatives they believe to be better than the alternative. At the same time, in the process of voting, they assert their acceptance of the outcome of the election. Those who are members of the inevitable "minority" in electorates have, therefore, voted both in favor of what they believe to be better and to accept what they believe to be worse.

There is a nonparadoxical way of describing this familiar behavior.

Persons who vote in an election consider the institution of elections and voting to be of more enduring value than the particular outcome of the election. Usually, this evaluation assumes some limits on the range of options presented in the electoral process. It also assumes the opportunity for reversal or realignment in future elections. And every democracy also provides safeguards and opportunities to counteract the results of any particular election result.

The analogy is evident. Any society that encourages or tolerates a range of plurality in the moral purposes of philanthropic agencies has decided that the institution of private philanthropy has a value that overrides the unavoidable harm that a particular philanthropic activity or program can do. Generally, there are tacitly or expressly recognized limits on the range of moral pluralism. There are also safeguards both in public oversight and, more importantly, in the philanthropy's exercise of its institutional responsibility.

The common sense of these safeguards requires no elaboration in theory. To a degree, they represent the experience of the craft, art, or practice of philanthropy. Accordingly, it is the experience of practitioners that is the source for their theoretical development. In the present context, it is relevant to indicate that some of these safeguards will articulate some of the arguments and evidence involved in the examination of the tension between moral pluralism and the common good.

Thus, some of the safeguards will involve a kind of political process of negotiation of consent among persons who will be affected by the philanthropic decision. Another recognized safeguard is the evaluation of any policy proposal from competing or conflicting perspectives before adoption. There are other ways of minimizing the risk of counterproductive policies, including the calculated seeding or support of contrary policy approaches.

To a degree, an examination of the relationship between moral pluralism and the idea of the common good sketches a theoretical analogue for accepted standards of practice. Perhaps its elaboration suggests some ways in which practice can be informed by the theoretical considerations that enter into a tradition, both ancient and modern, of reconciling pluralism with the common good.

Philosophy, Columbia University

PHILANTHROPY AND SELFISHNESS*

By John O'Connor

The question I want to discuss is "How can I say 'No' to a fund-raising appeal?" Since many people apparently find it easy to say "No," it is not clear what the problem is. Put briefly, the problem is this: I do not want to think of myself as uncaring, unfeeling, and insensitive to the needs of others. And yet, within the last year I have not responded to appeals for funds from a wide variety of causes: medical research, famine relief, freedom of speech, environmental protection. I have turned down requests for support of scholarly magazines, research institutes, and other good causes. My only moderate-sized contribution during that time has been to the capital campaign of an organization of which I am a member. I have enough to have made (very) small contributions to all of the organizations from which I received appeals, but not enough so that my contributions to any single cause would be of major significance. How can I justify not giving?

The problem arises because these appeals (some of them, at least) apparently put moral claims upon me: they say that people are suffering and have needs, and you can help to meet them. Or they say that the intellectual and cultural life of our society will be enriched if you help.

One traditional philosophic view holds that moral claims have a special status. They override political, economic, social, and other claims. The only thing, according to this view, that can free one from a moral claim is another moral claim. I can be absolved from an obligation to give to a charity if my resources are limited and I have a stronger moral reason to use my limited financial resources for another purpose, e.g., to save for my children's education. On this view, the only way I can be freed from the moral claims placed upon me by fund-raising appeals is to use my funds to support a cause that is even more morally worthy.

Yet there is something strange about this way of conceiving of the matter. Philanthropic activities are similar to supererogatory acts in that they are beyond duty. I may show myself to be a better person if I contribute, but I do nothing wrong, violate no moral norm, if I refuse to give. (I will not, in this

* I would like to thank Barbara Bellows, Martin Golding, my fellow participants at the Conference on Private Philanthropy and the Social Good, and the Editors of *Social Philosophy & Policy* for their helpful comments.

paper, deal with views that claim I have a moral obligation to give to charity.) It seems, according to this view, that my refusing to give, while not morally wrong in a strict sense, says something about me – that I am insensitive, hardhearted, indeed, that I am selfish. It is a comment on my character.

In his 1982 paper "Philanthropic Values," Robert Payton stresses the relation between philanthropy and character:

> To achieve and maintain a high level of philanthropy requires effort of intellect and effort of will. As individuals and as institutions we have still not accepted how difficult it is to do the right thing. We tend to be guided by an easy sentiment or by narrow rationalism. . . . Philanthropic activity at its best is then an informed discipline, a habit of mind and behavior infused with value.[1]

In this paper, I will propose the following thesis: In order to develop and maintain a character that is sensitive to the needs of others, a character that displays a philanthropic spirit, it is sometimes desirable and even necessary to harden one's heart – to refuse to respond to appeals for funds for good causes. This is not so much because only by doing so can we give to the causes we believe are really important, but because we need to affirm the integrity of our own set of values, of our own person.[2] There are so many good causes that if we try to respond to them all, we dilute our ability to make a difference to any. But more important is the fact that we dilute ourselves. We run the risk of losing touch with what is really important to us. We respond rather than act. We become an object that is vulnerable to manipulation rather than a person with "a habit of mind and behavior infused with value."

Of course maintaining one's integrity is not by itself sufficient to ensure that one is a concerned and sensitive person. We need, in addition, a commitment to the well-being of our fellow persons. But a person without integrity to values and standards, a person who may be guided by "easy sentiment or narrow rationalism," may also be guided by whim, by the feelings of the moment, and ultimately is vulnerable to becoming selfish in a truly negative sense if the pressures continually lead one in that direction. The habit of philanthropy can flourish in an effective way only if the person has a steady (not rigid) character that can persist over time, if the person has respect for himself or herself and for his or her values. If we value philanthropic people more than philanthropic acts, and I believe we should, then we must be prepared to pay a price: We have to learn to say "No," and we

[1] Robert Payton, "Philanthropic Values," paper delivered to a colloquium of the Woodrow Wilson Center, 1982.

[2] Bernard Williams discusses some of the issues related to this sort of claim in *Moral Luck* (Cambridge: Cambridge University Press, 1981).

have to learn to take "No" for an answer. And we have to respect that answer in those cases where the "No" is based upon an affirmation of the integrity of the person.

Taking "No" for an answer is relatively easy if the person tells us, for example, that he or she will not support our cause, a cause that we both believe is morally worthy, because the person has decided to contribute only to support of cancer research due to the fact that a close family member died of cancer. It is perhaps a bit harder to respect a person's decision to give only in support of the arts because the person likes the arts and believes they are important, especially if the cause for which we seek funds aims to alleviate human suffering, but at least we can see the concern the person has for bettering and enriching the lives of people, a concern that we share.

What is much more difficult to respect is a person's decision not to contribute if that decision is based upon values we do not share, for example, support of a cause we believe to be racist or otherwise morally unacceptable. In such a case, we may have to respect the person's integrity, but we can deplore and even work against the cause he or she supports. Respect for a person's integrity does not entail acquiescence in his or her policies.

But over and above all these, there is a case that must be considered: A person refuses our appeal for funds, not on the basis that the available funds are to be donated to another cause, but merely because the person does not think our organization is worthy of support. I believe that this case is important if we are to understand what it is for a person to affirm self-respect in the context of philanthropy. I will discuss this case in some detail later. In the meantime, the general point can be put this way:

> I affirm myself and my values not merely by deciding what causes are more worthy of support than others. I also affirm myself and my values by deciding what causes, including good causes, are not worthy of support.

My values are not merely "altruistic" or other-regarding. I value my own happiness and the happiness of those around me, and I have standards about how things should be done. My values include more than moral values, narrowly defined. Thus, respect for a person and a person's values, whether mine or someone else's, involves more than granting the person the right to act on his or her personal moral values, even if different from mine. It involves respecting decisions made on personal self-interested values, at least to the extent that these values help to maintain the coherence of the person. In fact, without healthy and active self-interest a person probably has little chance of developing an effective moral character. The point is that at times a person will refuse to contribute to a cause for a variety of reasons that seem to have nothing to do with moral concerns, indeed, for reasons that look selfish, and yet the refusal can be justified if we realize that in refusing the person is affirming the integrity and worth of his or her person and values. Only a person who is a whole person can develop and maintain a steady philanthropic character, and at times it may be necessary to act selfishly to be a whole person. To put the point as paradoxically as possible: sometimes a philanthropic person must act selfishly.

In what follows I will develop this theme. Along the way I will suggest an additional reason why it is vital that we respect the right of people to refuse to contribute, a reason that helps to clarify why philanthropy is such an important part of human life. I will begin by focusing on the often expressed view that Americans are too self-interested.

In a recent column in *The New York Times*, Leonard Silk writes about the tension between self-interest and civic spirit:

> Without love, benevolence and social concern to hold the society together, the pursuit of self-interest runs riot – and in increasingly dangerous directions. . . . China and the Soviet Union are looking for ways to improve their economic performance by relying less on public goals and more on motivating individuals and groups to pursue their self-interest. Does the United States require a shift in the opposite direction?[3]

Silk's central concern is with the paralysis that affects the nation's efforts to deal with the federal budget deficit, and thus his concern is with the opposition between self-interest and "civic spirit." Other writers have warned that we, as a nation, may be losing our concern not only for the common good but for individuals in need and for institutions that better the lives of citizens. Here the opposition would most appropriately be described as between self-interest (or selfishness) and altruism, rather than self-interest (or selfishness) and civic spirit. In both cases the tension is between selfishness or self-interest and something else.

First, it should be noted that the "self" in "self-interest" may not have a precise definition. If a person does not give to charity so that his or her children can have a larger inheritance, we see this as an extended version of self-interest. On the other hand, if a person contributes to a museum's fund to acquire or retain a significant painting, we tend to think of this as philanthropic and not self-interested. Yet in the former case it seems that the person is expressing concern for others, and in the latter the person may just want to have the painting nearby for his or her pleasure. Our intuitions suggest that children are more part of oneself than is a museum or a painting, but the boundary between self and others is not sharp.

[3] Leonard Silk, "Economic Scene," *The New York Times*, July 31, 1985.

Those who express concern that Americans are too self-interested seem to have one or both of two things in mind. They could mean, on the one hand, that there are pressing societal or group or individual needs that will not be met if people do not pitch in and help. If we look out only for ourselves or families or special interests, then we face a serious risk that certain policies, necessary for our well-being and perhaps even survival, will not be implemented. These people are concerned with the outcomes, and thus their view can be called "teleological."

On the other hand, they could mean that self-interestedness is morally unacceptable, at least as a general policy. They think we should care about others individually or collectively. Even if the government and wealthy foundations and corporations managed to meet human needs, we would not be fulfilling our obligations as persons if we did not express concern for others through philanthropic and charitable activity. This view we can call "deontological." Note that both or either of these views can be held no matter what one's stance is vis-à-vis religion. Both, in a broad sense, are moral views, and the difference in emphasis between them is that found between traditional teleological and deontological theories. In both cases, the enemy is the same: self-interest or selfishness.

Fund-raisers are acutely aware of the fact that even those who profess belief in the importance of philanthropy and who say that they believe people should give to good causes often do not, or at least do not give to the causes for which the fund-raisers labor. Sometimes this is because the potential donors have already decided to give all they can to other causes, but more typically the funds are there but the persons are hesitant. Here we get the typical fund-raising appeals: to guilt, to a sense of community, to self-interest, to fair play and reciprocity, and to the quality of the project. Fund-raisers are rhetors as much as reasoners; advertising techniques may work better than appeals to virtue or the worthiness of the cause.

So be it, many might say. If people will not give easily, then almost anything that gets them to give to a good cause is fair. Beat drums, cajole, encourage, offer premiums – do whatever is necessary. Just be glad, the cynic might say, that people can be led to contribute in this way, or many a good cause might suffer. So long as the cause is good and so long as the method of raising funds is not too outrageous, do not hesitate. If you need to enlist a famous person to endorse your cause, so be it. If people are willing to be used, take advantage of it. Of course, it would be a lot simpler if people, whether for teleological or deontological reasons, did not need to have arms twisted. But the world is as it is, and there is no use complaining. This "practical" or "cynical" view shares with the moral point of view the belief that the enemy is selfishness.

It might seem from all this that the morally conscientious person is faced with only two problems: "What's the maximum I can give?" and "To which causes should I give?" Yet we all know that matters are not as simple as these questions suggest. A conscientious person will be concerned with providing for his or her family, with saving for retirement, and, more to the immediate point, with having money for recreation and enjoyment. But how can this latter be justified morally, unless of course one can say that vacations are necessary to keep one's mental and physical health at peak – and this is necessary so that one can make more money that can be given to charity. There seems to be no room for self-interest for its own sake.

We are faced with a set of apparently legitimate moral considerations, whether we take them as creating responsibilities or not, that taken together and taken to their limit would tend to lead us to what seems to be an excessive and self-defeating sensitivity to the concerns of others. We need to know how we can with justification respond to this situation. I hope to show, by considering the case mentioned earlier, at least one sort of legitimate ground for refusing to contribute, a ground that is at least not obviously moral in basis. If I am successful I will throw a bit of light on the nature of philanthropy and the relation of philanthropy to selfishness.

The typical National Public Radio Campaign appeals to many things:

- You've listened, so give.
- You like us, so give.
- Here's a special show, so give.
- You can count on us, so give.
- We have these great premiums, so give.
- We want to do better than City X, so give.
- We have no advertising, so give.
- We have quality programming, so give.

The mix of appeals to self-interest and altruism (and other things) is impressive and, at least in the areas where I live and have lived, apparently effective. I suppose all of us have been tempted to contribute and many contribute regularly.

Since at least some of the reasons NPR stations give are moral reasons – You owe us, and we're a good thing for the society – the moral ball is in the listener's court. How can it be returned? (I am assuming the listener has enough on hand to make a contribution.) Rather than try to rebut those moral presumptions, I would like to try to justify one response that might override them.

"I choose not to give because the station isn't very good. It doesn't deserve my support." This sounds like "Your product isn't very good. I won't buy it," but there are significant differences. In particular, even if the station does not deserve my support, it does not follow that it does not deserve anyone's support. The reason depends upon the nature of what I will call "true philanthropy."

What does an individual contribution represent? Lots of things – values, altruistic tendencies, a sense of what the contributor can get out of it. What else does it involve? I believe that the act of contributing to a cause, if done thoughtfully and conscientiously, can be an extending of the self. Locke spoke of a person mixing his or her labor with a thing to create property rights. Individual philanthropy can do something like this. Individuals giving to an institution can identify themselves with it. They become part of it. Its fortunes are theirs. Its activities are theirs. This is more than merely supporting the cause because you find its goals compatible with yours or because you like it. It is becoming a part of the institution.

What makes this possible? First, philanthropy is voluntary. We do not have to give. Thus, in choosing, if we do it reflectively, we are expressing a part of our view of the world. We are saying "This matters to me."

But that is true of shopping for luxuries. We do not have to buy the product, but we do. The key difference is that philanthropy is not part of an exchange. We do not give in return for a service. It may be that some who contribute think they are paying for something either after or before the fact, but that is not really philanthropy. It is an economic transaction. True philanthropy may express a recognition of what one has received, but one owes nothing. It is a personal and not an economic activity. Thus I believe that, strictly speaking, there are no debts of gratitude, and that the term "debt" in this phrase is used metaphorically. Of course, it is possible for me to feel gratitude toward someone (e.g., a physician) to whom I also have a (financial) debt.

Then why isn't true philanthropy a matter of whim, of doing what one feels like – like going to the beach? Because it is (or should be) a serious matter. It involves our deep values about what is worth doing. It deals directly with basic human needs and with those things that are distinctively human. Because it is voluntary, noneconomic, and concerned with deep values, philanthropic activity tends to identify us with the cause we support. Of course one can identify with other things besides philanthropic causes. One can identify with family members. Fans identify with athletic teams. In addition, one can give to a cause without identifying with it. (I suspect much giving is of this sort). But when one contributes to an institution, one has a tendency to feel part of it.

Good fund-raisers know that if a person gives to an organization the person can be displaying a kind of loyalty, a commitment. He or she may become personally involved. I am not sure what connections exist between psychology and metaphysics, but I do believe that what one identifies with from a psychological point of view can make a difference as to who and what one is: one comes to think of the institution's fortunes as part of one's own fortunes. One feels with respect to it a range of emotions appropriate to oneself, e.g., pride in its accomplishments and shame at its serious failings. In traditional Chinese culture the individual conceived of himself or herself as an extended person – reaching back through time to encompass ancestors. In a similar way, we include family members and, I claim, some institutions as part of our extended selves. The act of contributing, while neither necessary nor sufficient for such identification, can have this effect.

Let us return to the example of the person who declined to give to the NPR station because it was not good enough. This can be an appropriate reason for not giving, because the person in the example views his or her contributing as a way of identifying with the station and refuses to identify with it. Of course, the person might have unreasonable standards. My point is only that the person's response has standing. It is an expression of personal integrity. A person can legitimately claim that a certain act is not going to be undertaken because to perform it is to compromise the self.

It might seem that it is probably a good thing, practically speaking, that not too many people think this way, because some cultural and other organizations might have trouble surviving. But for one who does think this way, the response is appropriate, not just to that person but to us.

However, even if this way of thinking were widespread and people could not in general be cajoled into giving by a mixed bag of altruistic and self-interested reasons, it would not follow that many organizations would be in trouble. As with our children, we can identify with things that are not perfect, that are developing, that have problems. So an amateur theater company or a storefront clinic might still receive funds from conscientious givers who chose to see themselves as part of the organization. But those who chose not to support such organizations could do so justifiably.

This may sound like a rationale for selfishness: "I'm better than that, so I won't contribute." This may be so, but only if an adherence to one's standards and values is selfish. Certainly the behavior looks selfish, for the organization does some good and I will not help. The key thing is the reason. If I will not give just because I do not want to, then I suppose I might be considered selfish in a mean sense. If I cannot bring myself to contribute because I cannot (do not want to) identify myself with that institution, then I have an appropriate kind of reason.

Why doesn't this affect all parts of our lives? Why is philanthropy special? Why shouldn't we refuse to play in, e.g., a playground basketball game, because we do not want to identify ourselves with its sloppiness?

Philanthropy plays a very special role in people's lives. At least it should. It is a major way of representing our recognition of other people as individuals with needs and potentialities, as beings worthy of respect. It expresses our membership in a moral community, not a community that we are forced to join, but one we freely join. It is the highest form of expressing our humanity. It gives us a chance to extend ourselves into the lives of others – to translate into action our most deeply held moral convictions.

Since philanthropy plays this role, it is tempting to say that a person who refuses to contribute to a worthy cause is selfish. Yet persons who say "No" can through that act be protecting the values that they hold. It is selfish only to one who believes that results (dollars contributed) are everything. People who do not reflect upon what is really worth doing or who let desires of the moment, even altruistic desires, move them in ways that their principles do not endorse are surrendering some of their autonomy. They are missing a chance to be full-fledged human beings.

Does this mean that people who refuse to contribute out of principle – including a principle of excellence – must take that money and give it to some other charity? No. There is no "must." But we can hope that people adopt values that will lead them to contribute to good causes. We can care very much that people care, but we have no right to criticize a conscientious person who refuses to respond to a request for a contribution on the ground that the cause is not one with which the person can identify. As fund-raisers we can hope either that conscientious people identify with what we do, or that we can get to them when their conscientiousness has slipped a bit. What we must acknowledge is the appropriateness of persons refusing to contribute on the grounds of protecting their integrity. This can be a spur to us to make our organization even better.

Philanthropy is by its very nature voluntary. If we treat fund raising as essentially a matter of persuasion, we debase the dignity that presumably forms a large part of the basis of our belief in the importance of philanthropic activity.

The fundamental point is this: to contribute to a cause can be to identify with it, and conscientious people have the right to refuse to so identify if they find the cause objectionable. The ability to identify or to refuse to identify with a cause is a part of what makes human beings distinctive, and the distinctiveness of human beings is what gives philanthropy its special importance.

The discussion thus far has focused on the individual. Can it be extended to institutions, e.g., foundations and corporations? This raises perplexing questions about whether and to what degree institutions can be taken to be similar to individuals. Rather than attempt to deal with these questions, I will limit my comments to the following point.

Just as individuals sometimes develop sets of priorities that put almost sole emphasis on results, there are foundations that like to fund projects that give results, especially the right results. In my sense, this is not true philanthropy at all. It is more like sub-contracting. That is, it is basically an economic relationship. These foundations are buying a product, or as close to the product as they can in conscience get. There is nothing wrong with this, so long as one does not confuse it with true philanthropy. One can hope for a result, or the right result, but one is not buying a result – one is supporting the people and their work. Perhaps our term 'philanthropy' is used a bit too broadly. If we called some of these other activities by the terms more appropriate, e.g., 'purchase' or 'contract,' then our consciences and our expectations would be clearer.

Thus far, the primary emphasis has been on the state of the potential donor and not upon helping those in need. Many of those familiar with fund raising could respond to my argument by pointing out that since the needs to be met are great, and since many people are unwilling to give, any means short of deception and physical coercion are appropriate to use in raising funds. Thus, while it may be acceptable for persons to refuse to give to causes to protect their integrity, it is equally appropriate for fund-raisers to use emotional and other appeals in an attempt to raise funds. If some people will not give unless they are invited to a fancy party where (other) important people are, invite them. If they will not give unless a friend asks them to give, get the friend to ask. (And if the friend will not ask unless cajoled, then cajole.) Since people often say "No," and since it is the responsibility of the fund-raiser to overcome the resistance, all (or almost all) is fair. After all, the needs are very great.

This response embodies the same spirit as the claim of those who support the constant growth of medical research and treatment. After all, they say, health and life are at stake, and the medical community would be open to moral censure if it did not do all it could to heal the sick and to save lives. Yet we all know that the matter is much more complex than this response suggests. Even if we set aside the avariciousness of some physicians, we see that the all-out pursuit of a good thing can have unfortunate consequences. Many have rebelled against the notion that we should do everything to keep people alive, because the quality of the life that is preserved is minimal. Others have charged that the emphasis on esoteric forms of treatment has reduced the ability of society to maintain the health of its citizens and the ability of both low (and middle) income people and the elderly to afford health care. Some talk about a crisis of health care. The general lesson is that even if a lot of talented and dedicated people commit themselves to achieving what all grant is a moral goal, the system can run aground and need reorientation and reform.

A similar problem has arisen in connection with political campaigning. Surely almost everyone believes in open debate and the right of citizens to support candidates of their choice. Yet our society has not yet worked out a satisfactory method of dealing with the economic dimensions of political campaigns. I believe the same is true of the current system of philanthropy. I will close by giving some examples of how this is happening.

First, not all fund raising falls within the bounds of moral appropriateness. There are cases in which someone owns a firm and invites those who do business with the firm to attend a fund-raising event in support of the owner's favorite charity. Those invited face a threat of losing business if they do not attend and make a (sizable) contribution. It is not clear how widespread this practice is, but what is clear is that while some of those invited may have chosen to contribute anyway and others may have contributed because a friend asked them, a number might contribute only because of the threatened loss of business. While some may call this "philanthropy," "extortion" seems a better term.

Second, the tradition of staging opulent events to raise funds can be challenged. Challenges to the current practice can be based upon the grounds that the money spent for food, flowers, hotels, and publicity could better be spent directly on the causes the events are intended to support, and that the funds raised through such events are typically directed to large and glamorous cultural institutions, thus reducing the amount available for less "attractive" causes. Although a number of people have expressed agreement with this challenge to the current way of doing things, those responsible for raising funds report that often people will not give without the enticement of an opulent social event. If this reflects a deep fact about human nature, then perhaps our society will have to learn to live with it; but just as people have learned to rethink the role of medical care in their lives, so too people may be led to reexamine their priorities concerning philanthropy. If people come to see themselves as agents whose philanthropic activity says a lot about themselves, then they may be willing to renounce or modify their vulnerability to the flattery embodied in the current system.

One suggestion that has been made is that in order to minimize information costs and cut down on the competition among philanthropic organizations, we should coordinate philanthropic activities either by political means or through voluntary associations.

Perhaps the government is the appropriate mechanism for meeting basic human needs. There is, however, much to be said for a system through which people can voluntarily help to meet such needs. The United Way is the best known example of a voluntary association of organizations that has reduced the competition among groups without reducing the amount contributed. Yet the United Way in some areas has developed a style of fund raising that has elements of coercion: employees of companies are sometimes not only encouraged to give, but it is suggested that divisions of companies that contribute less than others are somehow deficient, and statistics concerning how much is contributed by which divisions are sometimes made public. Thus, potential donors are not only encouraged to contribute, they are also subject to a form of intimidation if they do not. The result of such practices may be more money in the short run, but an increase in bitterness and a corrosive effect on those involved in the long run.

Third, some people are becoming hardhearted about charity because of the aggressive, insensitive, and intimidating practices of fund-raisers. Telephone solicitations have this effect on some people. The result may be not only that the causes represented by those doing the calling lose funds (although those who engage in the practice would probably claim that experience shows that "gentle" fund raising is less effective), but also that more and more people will out of frustration close their ears to all fund-raising appeals. Thus, the offensive practices of some may harm the even more deserving causes espoused by others.

Finally, the abuses of the current system are not directed only to those who are potential donors; they also can injure those who seek funds. The following case illustrates how our current system of private philanthropy makes it very difficult for some people involved in fund raising to defend the integrity of their own system of values.

Recently I was at a dinner with several people, including the president of a major art museum. This person talked extensively about the problems of raising funds. The audience was receptive because every person at the table was in one way or another a supplicant. He spoke of the need to mount a campaign against a proposed change in the tax laws that would affect charitable contributions. He mentioned other problems connected with fund raising. At the same time he evinced a real enthusiasm for the challenge. It was clear that he relished the opportunity to raise funds for a cause in which he believed so strongly.

Near the end of the dinner conversation he mentioned, almost as an afterthought, a frustration he had experienced. At the time it seemed of (relatively) minor significance, but the more I thought about it the more I realized that it was far from minor.

He said he knew when he took the job of president of the museum that he was assuming a large responsibility for fund raising. He knew that he would be expected to contribute financially himself and expected to spend a lot of time seeking contributions from others. This was a price he expected to pay. He knew he was asked to take the position because he had money, and because he knew lots of other people with money and had the ability to get some of it.

At the same time, he had reviewed his personal financial position and his personal philanthropic priorities and had decided that he would contribute to only four campaigns (one being that of his own museum). He felt that by so limiting his philanthropic activities, each of his contributions would be large enough to make a real difference. This carefully thought out plan was destroyed almost as soon as it was formed. As soon as he went to friends and acquaintances seeking funds for the museum, they felt free to approach him to get support for whatever cause they had adopted. He felt he had to give. As a result, his own contributions were much reduced in size and in impact. Thus, the sacrifice he had to make was not only in terms of his time and money. He had to sacrifice his own personal philanthropic commitments. Of course, he could resign the museum presidency, but he believes in doing what he can to help.

It is no help to suggest, which is probably why no one has, that such offices should be filled by people without means. Everyone knows that well-to-do people are more likely to contribute to an institution if they serve on its board, and they are more likely to have well-to-do friends who can be approached.

In a sense, then, these people are being treated as objects, as things that can get the funding job done. This is clearly objectionable, but a charge of immorality probably cannot ultimately be sustained if the person voluntarily chooses to accept the position, knowing what lies ahead. But it is unfortunate at the least and dangerous at worst if we permit ourselves to be caught up in a game in which we are willing to use people and to let them pay the price, including the assault on their ability to act upon their own values, all for a "good cause." The cause had better be pretty good, or we had better change the rules of the game.

It is not just the wealthy, influential, and concerned person who suffers – we all do. We become accustomed to thinking of potential donors as "objects" that we need to get at; and we begin to think of those who share our values and commitments in a similar way. This can erode the mutual respect that those who share a commitment to a cause should have. The financial rewards for the institution can be great; the insensitivity can be pernicious.

The problem the museum president described stems from a skewing of the ideal operation of a system of voluntary, private philanthropy. In theory (at least in my theory) the case for support of an institution should be made to individuals and foundations on the merits. One hopes the case will be successful. Whether it is or not will depend upon a number of factors, including the degree of overlap of the values that the institution espouses and that the potential donor has, the quality of the institution and its activities, and the extent to which the potential donor chooses to identify with the institution seeking funds. Each potential donor will make a personal decision on the merits of the case. In some instances the donor will have decided to limit contributions to, e.g., medical research and modern dance.

In fact, while this happens some of the time, the museum president's tale indicates that it is by no means universal. The wealthy fund-raiser approaches a wealthy friend. The wealthy friend makes a small contribution, perhaps merely because a friend is asking, and not because of any interest in the fund-raiser's cause. A year later the friend arrives raising money and the transaction is repeated. Both organizations have benefited, both participants have helped a friend, and both have lost some measure of control over their own personal philanthropic activity.

Some might say "Of course. Is there anything wrong with this? After all, everyone knows that's the game. If a person doesn't want to play, he or she shouldn't." But something is terribly wrong if those who are willing to help must pay a personal price for helping. We go too far if we encourage a system that works to impose heavy personal burdens upon those willing to help. Of course, the president could say "No" when approached by others who have contributed to the museum. But I gather this would have two unfortunate results: he would feel ungrateful and he might be much less successful at raising money. Thus, he has chosen to go along with the requests.

The basic problem can be identified by repeating a point made earlier, i.e., to contribute to a cause is ideally to make oneself part of it – to identify with it. If our system of philanthropy encourages us to contribute because we are intimidated or flattered or soothed, or even because a friend has asked us, or, as in the museum president's case, because of a fear that others will not support our cause if we do not support theirs, it does us a serious disservice. In such instances, we identify with things we do not believe in, or we lose the opportunity to identify altogether. The museum president saw this. His frustration was not at a minor inconvenience. He suffered an attack on his ability to translate his deeply held values into action.

Should we say that the attack on his values is merely an unfortunate side effect of his decision to raise funds? I hope not. Given the scale of fund raising and the fact that getting people to give is a difficult business, it is probably hopelessly utopian to propose the following, but here it is: the way we think about fund raising should be changed. We should expect to find, and should not resent it if we do, that people we have aided do not help us. We can hope, of course, that those who decline can justify their decision, that they can show why their values and their resources lead them in different philanthropic directions or no philanthropic direction at all. But the deeper point is one made in a different context by Flora Lewis: "The right to choose the good cause is as essential to freedom as the right of speech and peaceable assembly."[4]

---

[4] Flora Lewis, "The Choice of Causes," *The New York Times*, May 29, 1986.

Friendship, fair play, and gratitude are important moral notions, but they are misused when appeals to them undermine a person's carefully thought out plan of private philanthropy, for that plan expresses some of his or her deepest values, and destroying the plan renders the person incapable of translating these values into freely chosen action. The price is too high and to ask one to pay it precisely because one has chosen to work for a philanthropic cause is to create an incoherent and unacceptable situation. When philanthropy undermines philanthropy, something is seriously amiss. Perhaps nothing can be done, but there is a very good reason to try.

Philosophy, National Humanities Center

MORAL VALUES AND PRIVATE PHILANTHROPY

By Michael Hooker

My aim is to consider how private philanthropy – and that of foundations specifically – can better serve its social purposes. What I have to say may strike professionals in the field as naive. Admittedly my perspective is limited, for I have sat only on the grantee side of the desk. But I have also often tried to put myself into the grantor's frame of mind. The impressions gained in that way have been confirmed and modified by numerous recent conversations in preparation for this paper. The heads of foundations with whom I talked, the board members, and program officers, all were warmly forthcoming, forgiving of my naivete, and very helpful. I hope that what may be construed as criticism in what I have to say will not be taken as betrayal of those good offices. I mean it as support and encouragement of the positive intent I found in every instance.

When I accepted the invitation to write a paper on moral values and philanthropy, I first reflected on my own experience. I have often been troubled by my own moral standards in dealing with foundations. In nearly every instance, the proposals that I have written have contained an element of exaggeration – a heightening of the importance of the project I was proposing and of the capacity of my institution to carry it out. My end-of-grant follow-up reports have almost always contained exaggerated claims for the project's success.

This inflation was not done consciously. It was a tendency learned early in my career from reading other proposals and participating in committees designing projects to be proposed. That is to say, I came of age professionally in a cultural environment where such inflation was the norm.

It seemed to me that prudence required exaggerating my proposals in order to enhance the probability that they would receive favorable action, because I recognized that proposals competing with mine would be similarly exaggerated. It was as if we were all playing a game of rhetorical persuasion where the rules regarding honesty and candor are suspended or subtly altered, just as they are in poker. By the same token, I felt compelled to exaggerate my follow-up reports, because the probability of receiving future funding from the grantor would be diminished by candor. Whether either fear was justified is irrelevant; what is important is that I believed them to be.

It is also important that I believed that others believed the same. Indeed, I know from talking with deans and presidents that they believed future funding would be diminished by candor, and they believe it now. Once I began self-consciously to reflect on the element of deception in my proposals, I recognized that the whole culture of which I was a part supported such hyperbole.

In writing this paper, I attempt to discern how the forces that promote exaggerated claims can be altered to engender a higher level of honesty in proposal writing and grant reporting. Discussions with foundation representatives led me to recognize that there are substantial institutional or organizational impediments that must first be overcome. In these talks I also became aware of other institutional barriers to philanthropy being what it could be, and I want to address those as well.

As my ideas began to take shape I talked with a number of colleagues in other colleges about the themes of this paper. Many shared examples of misrepresentation in their own grant proposals and reports. I will use one of these as emblematic of the others, having changed the names for confidentiality.

John Ferguson is Dean of Arts and Sciences at a large, prestigious private university. One day he was informed by the university president that the head of the Munificent Foundation had indicated in conversation the likely receptivity of Munificent's board to a request for support of a curriculum reform effort. The president asked Ferguson to draft a proposal for the development of some new courses about which they had been talking – courses which would provide broader exposure to the major intellectual disciplines than the undergraduates normally receive. Ferguson knew that the university president and the head of the Munificent Foundation were close friends and that the university had received substantial support from the foundation in the past. For that reason, he knew that his proposal was likely to be accepted and that it should be particularly well written to reflect favorably on the university and on his boss.

In accordance with his discussion with the president, Ferguson drafted a proposal to enable faculty to design a set of new undergraduate courses. The proposal offered financial inducements to the faculty by giving them release-time and a large supplementary stipend. It also proposed supporting the best graduate students available at the university to serve as teaching assistants, and made liberal allowance for teaching materials, visiting lecturers, and expenses in the courses.

Ferguson was troubled by the fact that money received to support the graduate students would substitute for stipends that would be provided to them whether the program was funded or not. Similarly, the grant would substitute for visiting speaker funds that would otherwise be provided to the departments involved. Funds for instructional materials would be substitutive as well. Actually, it was only the funds for release-time and salary supplements that would otherwise not have been provided by the institution itself. Yet the faculty were normally obligated to design new courses without the benefit of release-time. Also, Ferguson did not think that the design of a few new courses would suffice to meet the need of curriculum reform, although he had been given to understand in his discussion with the president that such representation should be made. It was included in the proposal and it bothered him.

As expected, the program was funded by the Munificent Foundation, and it ran for three years. The first year was given over to planning and the last two years to implementation. At the end of the three years, Ferguson was asked by the president to draft a report to the Munificent Foundation.

The program, on balance, was a failure. While the courses were designed and taught as promised, student reaction was unfavorable: enrollments had declined substantially in the second year. Students complained that the courses were too narrow and technical – exactly the problems with the general curriculum which the courses were designed to correct. Ferguson and the president discussed the report and the embarrassment that would result from being candid about the results. Ferguson was told to soft-pedal the difficulties with the courses and to play up their benefits. His report ignored the decline in enrollments and emphasized the fact that the courses were academically rich and exciting to the instructors who taught them. He did not mention that the courses would not be taught in the future because of inadequate enrollment and the desire of the faculty, after the initial excitement, to return to their traditional courses. In deference to his boss and because he was worried about the possible loss of future funding from Munificent, Ferguson was satisfied to write a whitewashed report.

Reflection on this case reveals several institutional or cultural factors that contribute to the ethical problems involved. First, of course, is the desire of the university for funding and the belief that the proposal must be presented in the very best possible light. Second is the need of the university to underwrite its budget, and the opportunity provided by the grant for substitute monies. Third is the personal relationship between Ferguson's boss and the head of the foundation, a relationship that would be injured by the university's failing to fulfill its promise with respect to the grant. Fourth is the desire on the part of the foundation to support distinguished institutions which it has good reason to believe will spend the monies wisely. Fifth is the fear on the part of the university that an unfavorable report on the grant might jeopardize future funding. Sixth is the tendency of the grantee to "tailor" its proposals to the guidelines or interests of the grantor. Finally, the case raises questions about a foundation's responsibilities for due consideration before a grant is made, for monitoring the project under way, and for assessing its results. The case poses even larger questions involving support for specific programs versus unrestricted support for institutions.

Let me focus on the phenomenon of inflation in proposals and final reports. It led us into the other problems; possibly its solution will lead us out. We will find that institutional forces – forces endemic to the current culture of foundation philanthropy – serve to perpetuate the phenomena of exaggerated proposals, suppressed failures, and a general lack of candor in grantee communication with grantors.

It might at first blush appear that there is nothing really "wrong" with the exaggerations we have identified, that proposal writing and grant reporting adopt by custom a special kind of persuasive rhetoric. Where's the harm? Program officers and foundation boards were not born yesterday; they know full well that the grantee is trying to sell his program and his institution. There is probably substantially less outright fraud in grantsmanship than in society as a whole. The system works to ensure that much good is done, so why tinker with it?

It is probably true that little direct harm comes from grantee-perpetrated deception. Still, there are compelling reasons to seek its elimination. In the first instance, there is something unsettling in the idea that a condition of less than honesty is something we should live with. It belittles us all to suppose that telling and being told white lies is simply part of our culture. White lies are still lies. It is not excessive moralizing to maintain that accepting innocent lies in one arena of society functions to encourage deception elsewhere, further lowering the integrity of our society as a whole.

Moreover, and more importantly, philanthropy as an institution has an obligation to achieve a level of integrity well above that of society in general. The overriding purpose of the institution of philanthropy is to improve the world in all its aspects, particularly those that pertain to values. This purpose cannot be accomplished well if philanthropic agencies do not themselves exemplify the highest ideals and values.

If we are to reduce the frequency and magnitude of exaggeration in proposals and reporting, as I hope the reader believes we should, then the burden of promoting that change must rest with the foundations themselves. That "must" is a prudential obligation, not a moral one. Morally it is no more incumbent on foundations to promote candor than on grant seekers to do so. After all, it is the grant seekers who are directly responsible for the shortcomings we are focusing on. The problem is that moral admonition alone is unlikely to change the behavior of grantees. As long as they perceive candor to be reducing the probability of being funded, they will not be fully candid. Grantees collectively can hardly bring about reform while sensing that it is in their individual interests to resist such reform.

We have to look to the grantors for the mechanisms that will correct the problems. Individually and collectively, foundations have the capacity to change the culture in which grants are sought and reported. If you have any doubts, you have only to recall how attentive each of us has been to the slightest nuance in our dealings with prospective donors. Even so, this cultural change will not come easily. It will require the concerted effort and attention of foundation boards, presidents, and, most importantly, foundation program officers. Most of the weight will fall on the shoulders of already overworked program officers because it is they who are in direct contact with grantees, and it is primarily through direct contact that change will come about. It is only when grantees perceive that forthrightness is the best policy – that it is the foundation's policy – that they will become honest in their representations. It will fall to the program officers to convince them; and for this to occur, there will have to be substantial changes within the foundations themselves.

It is easy to understate the difficulty of enhancing candor and reducing hyperbole. Hyperbole is ubiquitous in our society. It bombards us daily through television and print advertising. We in academe contribute through our admissions and alumni publications. It is so commonplace for sports information offices to exaggerate the exploits of our teams that we do not even think of such "color" as objectionable or as contributing to the spread of hyperbole elsewhere.

The problems are exacerbated and their solutions more difficult because we also live and work in a cultural context of adversarial relationships; secrecy and deception are one way of interacting with each other. It is so easy to see ourselves in a win-lose contest with the institutions of society and with each other. When combined with the grant seeker's belief in the worth of his cause and his conviction that it should therefore be supported by the foundation of choice, the broader context of adversarial relationships promotes truth-stretching in proposals. Foundations, in their relationship with grant seekers, can create a countercurrent to even such broad cultural forces by not acting in accordance with them and by encouraging their clients to follow suit.

This countercurrent can flow only from a foundation culture in which candor is engendered and esteemed, in attitude and in organization. We can safely assume the intent of foundations in principle. Therefore, I can think of nothing more effective in this regard than a substantially improved quality of communication between the foundations and their clients.

Foundations, speaking broadly, could be more open in sharing information about their philosophies, goals, programs, and procedures. They could also be more open regarding their own misgivings about their philosophies, goals, programs, and procedures. For foundations operating in the public trust, to open themselves to public scrutiny in all respects, including their own misgivings, would do wonders as an antidote to societal secrecy, mistrust, and misunderstanding.

One of the first places for foundations to practice such openness and candor is in the president's letter and the annual report. Another opportunity for continuous candor is in the interaction of program officers with grantees. In a way that I will address in a moment, program officers are constantly under political seige; of necessity they have become defensive in their dealing with grantees. To risk dismantling these defenses, program officers will need the full support and backing of their presidents and boards.

There are forces that operate in opposition to open and honest communication between program officer and grantee. One of these forces results from a tension between the program officer's responsibility to assure that the goals and expectations of the foundation are met and the necessity of his working to help produce a program or project that the grantee and his organization are interested in bringing about. The programs, goals, and guidelines of the foundation rarely reflect the interests of grantees exactly. It is a challenge for the program officer to get the grantee to work toward the guidelines. The more specific the goals and guidelines, the stronger the nudge has to be. This tension contributes to the adversarial character of the relationship. It would be better for all concerned, I think, if program officers had more discretion in interpreting the guidelines of the foundations. While being given more latitude to negotiate with grant seekers, the program officer should at the same time be given a mandatory responsibility to report on what he has done. Until such open negotiations are permitted, the undermining tendencies at work will be concealment by the grant seeker and rationalization by the program officer.

The program officer's inclination to be straightforward is diminished by a kind of bunker mentality inherent in being on the firing line. Not all grant seekers are powerless in the relationship between themselves and foundations. Because the program officer says no to grantees so often, eventually he is sure to catch some flak. It usually comes from the trustees of the grantee organization who complain to the president or members of the foundation board about the program officer. The complaints may not be justified, but they create a psychological pressure on the program officer. The result is a tendency to duck the responsibility for saying no.

As an untoward aspect of career development, the program officer begins to use dishonest techniques for saying no. For example, he will claim that a particular proposal "doesn't fit the guidelines" or that it is "not expressive of the interests" of his trustees. Persistent use of this device creates a psychology of estrangement from grantees. It takes an enormous amount of fortitude to say no directly. It is unreasonable to expect individual program officers to sustain the courage of the Lone Ranger. Part of the fortitude has to be provided by the president and the board. Their program officers must be sheltered by a whole foundation culture directed toward conditions of honesty and openness in all relationships.

Once the culture begins to change, there is likely to be a reinforcing synergism – in the area of personal relationships, for example. Because they fear program officers and feel they must seduce them with beauty while concealing their flaws, grant seekers do not pursue a relationship with program officers built on trust. Grantees are reluctant to question the judgment of program officers for fear of engendering the officers' disdain. The program officer who hears nothing but flattery from grantees, nothing critical of his judgment, naturally yields to a sense of omniscience and omnipotence, which at some level even the program officer knows is not warranted. Once this phenomenon is dispelled by a more candid relationship, the program officer and the grantee will feel less estranged from each other. The job of each should become much easier and their joint effort enjoyable.

Beyond this critical personal relationship, let us consider a deep-seated psychological and sociological phenomenon that tends to perpetuate attitudes of deception toward the self and others. It is one that is present in any organization, and it is an aspect of our individual psyches. Applied to foundations, it is represented by the fact that what a foundation holds at any given time to be important for the foundation to address – its area of priority concern – can in actuality be a kind of indigenous artifice. A foundation's interest at any given time will have arisen from discussions within the staff, within the board, and between the two regarding the issues of the day. Once an area of particular concern has been delineated for attention, the problems associated with that area tend to take on a greater significance within the foundation than they had when they were simply some among many large problems being considered. It follows that the importance of projects aimed at those problems begins to grow in the minds of people associated with the effort.

Initially there may have been open skepticism; subsequently it tends to be suppressed. What skepticism remains becomes a shared feeling rather than a subject of conversation. Growing enthusiasm for the direction the foundation has taken tends to drive out doubts about its capacity to achieve significant results in that direction. A conventionalization of belief emerges that is mutually supportive and rejects contrary views and evidence. The foundation's vision becomes afflicted by a myopic optimism.

Francis Sutton, who is doing a history of the Ford Foundation, speaks of a "conspiracy of optimism" that arose during the period in the 1960s when an important part of Ford's effort was directed toward improving governance in several African nations. The "conspiracy" arose from a strong desire to achieve something important. On the reasonable belief that formal training in public administration would affect in a significant way the quality of government in African nations, Ford devoted a great deal of effort to providing such training. Confidence was supreme as the program got under way. Mounting enthusiasm drove out doubts. Contrary evidence that was available on the likely success of the program was not perceived in the way that, in retrospect, it should have been. During a fairly short time in the 1970s, the Ford staff's confidence totally collapsed on the realization that the program was a failure. It was analogous to a paradigm shift in science. Once people's apperception had been transformed, much of what earlier should have been seen as contrary evidence came into focus.

Nor are individuals immune to this phenomenon of illusion. As a historian of philosophy, I have often found myself becoming more and more convinced of a particular theory the harder I tried to explain and defend it to someone else. In making our views intelligible to others, we tend to suppress the uncertainties that we might entertain while those views are being formed, to filter out any vagueness in our own understanding. The necessity of having confidence in what we are talking about tends to drive out reasonable doubt. We, as individuals or as organizations, simply cannot live comfortably with misgivings and doubt. We are not at ease with this aspect of being human.

To pursue the phenomenon just a little further, I think it is obvious that something similar frequently occurs with a breadth that is national. This is part of what subtends the phenomenon of fashion in Zeitgeist. I have been amused for some time to watch the waxing and waning of investor interest in biotechnology. A few years ago, absolutely astounding forecasts were made for biotechnology's effect on our lives and on business and commerce by the year 2000. The forecasts were simply earth-shattering – and all of the theoretical evidence to support them was right there. An enormous movement of investor interest followed the forecasts. Two and one-half years later it was clear that the favored biotechnology companies had been consuming all of the investment money available to them at a very rapid rate. Investors began to demand the promised products. When they were not forthcoming, the retreat began in earnest.

In the greedy frenzy that fueled the public offerings of the first biotechnology companies, investors had ignored admonitions that products would not be forthcoming quickly. To the extent that they understood the complexity of the science involved, investors overlooked obvious problems that had to be solved before there could be commercially useful products. Early enthusiasm drove out doubt. Later, too late for some, doubt drove out enthusiasm.

The phenomenon I have described – let us call it myopic optimism – makes it difficult for foundations to look critically at large priorities and programs. In its individual manifestation, it makes it especially difficult for program officers and for grantees to look critically at how favored programs might fail. In thinking through his proposal, the grant seeker naturally subordinates his doubts about its success. They have all but disappeared when it comes time for putting thoughts to paper. This shoring up his beliefs, this myopic optimism, enables the grant seeker to marshal arguments and enthusiasm with which he can parry any questions. or misgivings the program officer may raise. Of course, once the program officer becomes convinced, the myopic optimism begins its work on him as well. In advocating the proposal to his colleagues, the program officer will automatically discount the respect merited by any doubts that may be raised.

There is another phenomenon of the human psyche that exacerbates the problem of myopic optimism – our aversion to complexity. Most of us, though not consciously as a rule, are willing to deceive ourselves in order to avoid the discomfort of living with ambiguity and facing a complexity that taxes our capacity to cope. We would much prefer to have our problems and their solutions framed in absolutes; decisions would be so much easier as either/or alternatives. The doubts that may appear around the edges of something we want or need to do are a complication to be put aside.

This aversion to complexity is evident not only in the grant seeker's proposal and in the foundation's consideration of its interests and programs; it is also present in virtually every aspect of our individual and collective lives. At the national level, the media favor this desire for simplicity by cleansing world problems of their complexity. Solutions to the world's big problems tend to look a little simpler immediately following the evening news. This consistent lack of sensitivity to the political, economic, and moral complexity of the world is one more element eroding the quality of international understanding.

Foundations are bound to encounter complexity because, to begin with, they do not have the bottom line of business or a comparable finite standard against which to set their objectives and measure results. Foundations must consider a multiplicity of objectives. Many of them will be long-range ones. A multiplicity of distant objectives is guaranteed to breed uncertainties and produce complexities. The foundations' response is a kind of subjectivity leading to unrealistic goals, poorly designed programs, and a failure to assess adequately a program's results.

For example, the foundation that sets out to improve the food supply in Ethiopia will be confronted with a challenge of such breadth and having so many facets as to be almost incomprehensible in its true complexity. Given our aversion to complexity and the inclination toward myopic optimism, the natural tendency will be to solve those problems which, in the design of the idealized program, seem amenable to solution. Attention to those problems which seem hopelessly complex will simply evaporate in the dry desert air. The end result may very well be the illusion that when several problems have been solved, they all have. The illusion of composition I have described as a problem for foundations is a phenomenon that can beguile any organization.

Let us return to some specific things that foundations can do to improve their cultural environment. One of the most important advances foundations could make is instituting a sophisticated system for review, a kind of due diligence before grants are made coupled with systematic post-grant evaluation. Good evaluation is expensive, and foundations will have to overcome the psychological hurdle of committing substantially more resources to administration. I think there is delusion in believing that every dollar that goes to projects rather than to administration is a dollar better spent. My own experience and numerous confirming conversations lead me to believe that it is simply not the case that foundations have the capacity to discern worthy projects and ensure their adequate implementation without a lot of administrative oversight. Even the best institutions, whether grantor or recipient, sometimes have unnecessary or poorly run programs. Without thorough accountability, the probability of that happening is bound to increase.

Before a grant is made, there should be adequate time and funds for the program officer to do on-site reviews and to bring in outside consultants for on-site reviews. Before a proposal is approved, substantial time should be spent with the grantee to ensure that the program is well-conceived and that it is likely to be carried out as portrayed in the proposal. To the fullest extent possible, quantifiable measures of effectiveness should be established before the grant is made. There needs to be a mechanism for periodic monitoring and reporting that is simple, clearly understood by the grantee, and used consistently by the grantor. Such procedures, of course, will increase the expense to the grantee and compensation should be built into the grant.

The foundation should see its interest as intimately bound up with that of the grantee in ensuring a project's success. The atmosphere sought should be that of a joint venture. While this relationship may suggest undue intrusiveness on the part of the foundation, that need not happen. Openness in communication between the program officer and the foundation, on the one hand, and the grantee organization and its officers, on the other, can mitigate any feeling of unwelcome intrusion. Even a friendly monthly telephone call between the program officer and the grantee officer in charge of the funded project is likely to be sufficient in an atmosphere of candor and cooperation.

While pre-grant evaluation and the monitoring of implementation should be primary responsibilities of the foundation staff, I think it is important that post-grant evaluation be performed by disinterested outside parties. There is a built-in conflict of interest if the foundation evaluates its own work. The foundation, having a stake in the success of its funded projects, will tend to overlook failures, especially those that are not immediately apparent. There will be a similar tendency for the foundation staff to overestimate the degree of success.

Projects should be evaluated against the original suppositions that led to the award of the grant; and they should also be evaluated against values that may have emerged as the project developed. While it may not have accomplished exactly what was originally intended, the project may well have succeeded in accomplishing something wholly desirable even if unintended or unanticipated. Evaluators should also be encouraged to question the foundation's intent in funding the project and the value of the project in this broader context.

Thorough, consistent evaluation of grants will enable a foundation to refine its own pre-grant evaluation procedures by realizing, for example, what questions it should have asked and did not. It will also be able to refine its own goals and objectives by seeing what did and did not work in a program it helped to shape.

After the evaluation is complete and a report submitted, the report should be discussed jointly among the foundation, the grantee, and the evaluator. To the extent that objective measures of evaluation can be used, it is important to use them; but it is probably more important to have the kind of subjective evaluation that an expert is able to deliver. It is especially important that the subjective aspects of the evaluation be discussed among all the parties involved. This kind of attention to evaluation will substantially enhance the quality of integrity in the whole culture of philanthropy. It provides an atmosphere of responsibility, concern, and communication.

I said earlier that foundations can substantially enhance the atmosphere of candor in communication by sharing information about their own deliberations concerning their programs, goals, and objectives. One way to do this is for the foundation to evaluate formally its own programs. Again, such evaluation should be performed by outside disinterested parties. One of the difficulties will be finding disinterested parties who are sufficiently knowledgeable in the field. Especially for a large foundation with broad influence, it could be difficult to find experts who do not stand to benefit in some way from the foundation's programs. It will be one more task for the president to balance the expertise of prospective evaluators against their likely objectivity.

Evaluation of the foundation's programs should look first at the mechanism used to establish the foundation's own priorities, goals, and objectives.

The evaluation should not only proceed grant by grant, but should also consider the effectiveness of entire programs, starting with the procedures for the review of proposals. It would doubtless prove useful to go back and look at earlier programs and projects from the perspective of five or ten years later, helping to provide a more realistic assessment of current directions and interests. In the desire to do something new and innovative, the experience of the past can easily be neglected. That risk is less likely if a foundation is self-consciously reflecting on its experiences of the past decade, counteracting the myopic optimism that grows with time.

I want to turn now to consideration of a broad area we might label "the purpose of philanthropy." I want to raise some questions about the kinds of programs a foundation ought to adopt. In my own view, foundations should be more willing than they tend to be to take risks on programs that are not sure things.

One of the reasons that grant seekers tend to dissemble is that they believe, from pretty sound logic, that foundations do not want to fund programs that have an appreciable probability of failure. It is true, as my discussions with foundation board members have led me to believe, that foundations want to be bold, innovative, and at the cutting edge of world problems – just as long as the proposals served up to them are guaranteed. They want such proposals, understandably, because they want to be sure that their money is not wasted; and they want cutting-edge proposals so they can believe that the money was well spent for progress. More often than not, however, it is caution rather than boldness that guides foundations' selection of proposals to fund; they can be likened more to commercial bankers than to venture capitalists.

While foundations are no longer bold risk takers for the most part, they tend to see themselves in that light. That they perceive themselves mistakenly tends to diminish the probability that they will in fact be bold and innovative. This caution is often reflected in program guidelines that are written and goals that are set in such a way as to preclude failure – an insurance policy that covers both the foundation and its grantees against risk.

That so few foundations thoroughly evaluate the programs they support suggests that, in truth, they do not see themselves as risk takers. In an earlier incarnation, George Schultz once said that if 65 percent of your efforts are successful, you're a genius. I would guess that if a foundation's board discovered that only 65 percent of its efforts were successful, it would regard itself as a failure.

It will require bold leadership by the trustees and president to make a foundation's program officers bold. The program officers should be encouraged to take risks, and never punished for doing so. They should contribute their share of failures, which is evidence of risk taking and shows that the foundation is in vigorous health. This will be true provided that the riskier a foundation's ventures, the more thorough its evaluation becomes. Evaluation should be regarded as a way to improve future performance, not merely a way to tally the score.

One aspect of risk taking that foundations should support is proposals that come over the transom. Foundations should be willing to break out beyond the grantee organizations they know and trust; they should be known to welcome proposals from new and little-known organizations. There is, of course, the initial time and expense of working with someone the foundation does not know, and the higher probability of error. However, that is the cost of risk which becomes lower as the foundation increases its attention to evaluation and monitoring.

Having said that foundations should be risk takers, I also want to argue that they should devote more resources to institution building than they do. These are difficult times for all nonprofit organizations. For many, just coming close to the break-even point is a mark of success. Foundations have the opportunity to make a difference at the margin by providing the critical increment of funding that will enable existing programs and institutions to remain strong through these difficult times. Because foundations work by setting goals, they prefer to invest in projects rather than institutions. But these are different and critical times. Institutional funding is essential to sustain the core programs of institutions. Without this structural stability, all of those appealing ancillary projects are vulnerable to failure.

I do not mean to suggest that foundations should simply give general operating revenues or endowment funds and walk away. The foundation must feel it is genuinely a part of the institution's success. The institution must know that it is not simply being given unrestricted funding with fiduciary concern. Here, at the highest levels within the foundation and its grantee institutions, is the opportunity for the two to work together in planning, monitoring, and assessing how the committed funds are working for institutional stability and achievement.

Much of the institutional-support funding that I have seen in the past has not been particularly well managed by the recipient. In order to encourage efficiency, a foundation should stipulate the control of its money, making it completely clear to both parties how the funds will be used and how they will be monitored. This commits the institution as a whole to stewardship, while allowing some latitude to adjust as needed. Closely watched in this way while proceeding with a sense of partnership, most institutions will respond with exemplary responsibility – which is another and more positive aspect of institutional funding that I have seen.

A countervailing force to the willingness of a foundation to provide core support is its understandable and strong desire to be an agent of change.

However, foundations must recognize that they are a different kind of player now than they were before government involvement in large-scale social spending. They tend to think that they should be solving global problems and that their effects are much greater than they are. Foundations must be willing to recognize their limitations. Philanthropy is a miniscule portion of the money spent annually on social needs in this country alone. For that reason especially, foundation dollars, in order to make a difference, have to be used to fund programs on the margin.

While I have argued that foundations should be willing to provide core support, I am equally emphatic in urging that programs and project funding should be gambled on projects that government is not likely to undertake. It is this dual endeavor of strengthening the core while reaching out to keep pace with change or be ahead of it that represents in my view the ideal use for social venture capital, an ideal and essential investment in society.

Philosophy, University of Maryland – Baltimore County